Nakedness

2013

NAKEDNESS
Stories of God Stripping Away the Chaos and the
Mundane to Reveal Truth and Light Within
Copyright © 2013 Sandra Kristen Moore
www.sandrakristenmoore.com

Published by:
Blooming Twig Books
New York / Tulsa
www.bloomingtwig.com

Cover photograph (of Sandra Kristen Moore's feet)
by Elizabeth Anne Moore

All passages from the Bible were excerpted from the
New International Version, unless otherwise noted.

Any information or opinions expressed herein
do not necessarily reflect the views of the publisher.

All rights reserved. This book may not be photocopied for personal or professional use. No part of this book may be reproduced, stored in a retrieval system, or transmitted in any form or by any means (electronic, mechanical, photocopying, recording, or otherwise) without permission in writing from the author and/or publisher.

Paperback: ISBN 978-1-61343-040-8
eBook: ISBN 978-1-61343-041-5

First Edition

Printed in the United States of America.

For my best friend,
my biggest fan, my love, my husband Rob.

To the Reader,
that my journey may encourage you on yours.

Nakedness

Stories of God Stripping Away the Chaos and the Mundane to Reveal Truth and Light Within

Sandra Kristen Moore

BLOOMING TWIG BOOKS
New York / Tulsa

Table of Contents

INTRODUCTION 13

ONE: NAKED 19
Promiscuous 21
Drunk 25
Love 30
Fear 37

TWO: STEPS 43
Secrets 45
Bliss 48
The Gate 50

THREE: IT'S NOT ABOUT ME 53
Active 55
Clarity 58
Perception 61

FOUR: ENCOURAGEMENT 65
Atta Girl! 67

FIVE: OBJECT 71
Captive 73
Talents 76
Pause 79

SIX: CHASING 83
Stop, Pray and Follow 85
Pursuit 87
Be Still 90

SEVEN: INSTRUCTIONS 95
Humble Pie 97
Obedience 100
Disguised 103

EIGHT: FOR GOD 107
Jesus 109
Trumpets 112
Puzzles 116

NINE: LIKENESS 121
Ordinary 123
Grace 126
Preservation 129

TEN: THE UNSEEN 133
Magic 135
Blessings 138
A Moment 141

ELEVEN: FASTING 145
Control 147
God's Feast 150
Cravings 154

TWELVE: HARD PILL 159
Teachable 161
Extra 165

THIRTEEN: LEAP 171
Mine 173
Eye Contact 176
Discomfort 179

FOURTEEN: JUSTIFIED 183
Excuses 185
"In" Crowd 188
Elevating 191

FIFTEEN: SHOULDERS 197
Disciples 199
Hit 202
Proficiency 206

SIXTEEN: DEFINED 211
Balance 213
Intimacy 217
Bullied 220

SEVENTEEN: REVELATION 225
Overcomer 227

AFTERWORD 235
ACKNOWLEDGMENTS 239
CONCORDANCE 243
ABOUT THE AUTHOR 247

Introduction

My name is Sandra Moore. People may tell you that I am a loving, adoring wife, a caring mother of four, the oldest of three, a devoted daughter, a good friend, a prayerful sister in Christ, and a child of God. But I am actually far from the perfect picture these words paint.

In the past I have worked hard to maintain this lovable image to all, at the cost of my relationship with God. But now, my relationship with the Lord has become intrinsic to who I am.

I write so you can see that I am really an unfaithful wife, a crazed and frustrated mother of four, the most prideful of three, a disrespectful daughter, a forgetful friend, a judgmental sister in Christ, but still a child of God. Maybe you can relate to one, two, or all of these. Maybe you can't relate to any of them, but have the same deep desire as I did, to find out how to quench that yearning for something more that burns inside of you. This book has tales of all of that.

Nakedness

As I pondered what to call this book of stories, I had a conversation with my husband about lying naked, and that's when it struck me. I thought about how exposed and vulnerable and sometimes shameful I feel when I am naked, because there is nothing to hide the flaws of my body—it's all out there for my husband to see. This is how God wants me to live my life—not physically naked, but completely, emotionally, and spiritually exposed.

In Genesis chapters 2 and 3, Adam and Eve lived in the beautiful garden with everything their hearts desired, including their intimate relationship with God. They were naked and unashamed (Genesis 2:25), and had no need unmet. The only rule was that they could not eat the fruit from the tree that was in the middle of the garden. So they went about in paradise until one day Eve was tempted to eat of this fruit, and she did, giving some to Adam too. As a result: "The eyes of both of them were opened, and they realized they were naked; so they sewed fig leaves together and made coverings for themselves." (Genesis 3:7).

They had everything they could ever need, yet sought more. And it was through their desire to have *more* that they ended up naked, ashamed, and trying to cover themselves up.

I can relate to this nakedness, because this is what I do every day. I often want *more* than what I have, and in order to *get* more, I feel an increasing need to cover myself up with all of the day-to-day aspects of my life. Adam and Eve used fig leaves to cover up their nakedness. I cover myself with both the "mundane" and "chaotic" elements of my life.

The word "mundane" defines my daily maintenance—laundry, dishes, cleaning—the things I do over and over again. These mundane tasks are things that have to get done, but are very hard to find joy in. It is very easy to cover my "nakedness" and hide here, behind these tasks when I am bothered by something, and when life is not going the way I planned. I can get lost in the mundane for hours at a time, as I do one mindless chore after another.

The irony is that "mundane" has another definition I wasn't aware of until recently. Yes, the word means, "to do something that lacks excitement," but it also implies something that is of the "earthly world," and not a "heavenly or spiritual one." How appropriate that definition feels to the mundane tasks of my daily routine. Too often, I let these mundane, earthly tasks cover any spiritual aspirations within me. And when the mundane isn't a sufficient concealer of my nakedness, I turn to the chaos.

"Chaos" is the other word that describes my life. I run from place to place, carting children, doing errands, attending sporting events and practices, on the go all the time. I often feel like I can barely keep my head above water, trying not to drown in all the busy-ness.

It's this self-created chaos that easily covers up any good work God is doing in me. Instead of focusing on God, I think only about the crazy tasks at hand. I overcommit to do more than I have time for, out of an overwhelming desire to please others. This, of course, creates the perfect setting for me to show how I can do it all—right before I secretly fall on my face trying.

This book is about exposing yourself, and becoming uncovered before God, peeling back the layers of the mundane and the chaos in your life, as I try to do each day in mine. It is time for us to stop hiding and covering ourselves, and to let the world see who we truly are.

This book is written in two sections: I begin with my shady past, because in order for you to understand how wonderfully God has worked within my life, you have to see how things have changed. The second section is about the person I am becoming through God's daily stripping of the mundane and chaos.

In 2005 God started to open my eyes through things I read and people I encountered—helping me begin to realize that I didn't have to hide my imperfections anymore. Since then, I have been learning that every one of my experiences brings me closer to God. Each one offering insight into how my attempt to be "perfect," leaves no necessity for God and no way for Him to show how valuable He is in my life. But it is only with the knowledge of Jesus' love for me that I would have the courage to share these experiences.

Here I have laid out who I have tried to be of my own accord— a "good" wife, mother, daughter, sibling, friend, Sister in Christ, Child of God. Sometimes I have covered the unpleasant and plastered on a smile. Other times I have faked it and made it believable. And still other times I have hidden behind the mundane and amongst the chaos.

In this book, I share the attempts that I have made to open the closed doors and reveal what's really inside, allowing more of the real me to be seen. I share how God has used each struggle, adventure, joy, tear, pain, trial, chaotic and mundane moment to strip away the barriers I try to hide behind.

My prayer is that you will find hope and rest in the Lord, as I do, and that He will help you to shoulder your burden, as you travel through the mundane and chaotic days of your life.

- Sandra Moore, April 2013

One
Naked

Praise be to the God and Father of our Lord Jesus Christ, the Father of compassion and the God of all comfort, who comforts us in all our troubles, so that we can comfort those in any trouble with the comfort we ourselves have received from God.

2 Corinthians 1:3, 4

Promiscuous

I lost my virginity when I was fourteen. I was dating a senior in high school, and I was a freshman. It was in my own bed, which you would think would make it more comfortable, but it didn't. It was a painful experience. Something I wasn't sure I ever wanted to do again.

I had gone through the obscure videos in elementary school that explain how your body changes and what sex is. If you remember these videos and the awkwardness of them, then you'll know why I had blocked them from my mind.

I don't remember my parents talking to me about sex. They both worked, and since I was the oldest child, I was allowed a great amount of freedom and independence. They seemed to think I wouldn't do anything that would cause them concern.

And I didn't think much about God, as I saw Him as someone only talked about if we went to church. That left me with my curiosity, what I saw in movies and television, and what others thought, to figure out what sex was. So when this first opportunity arose, I thought, "Why not?

Despite the discomfort and pain, after my first time, it became something I did do again and again. Sex became my attempt to feel worthy; to soothe the longing I felt deep down in my soul.

I also thought it would bring excitement to my life. But it didn't do any of these things.

My sophomore year, there was a boy who I was head over heels for. When he finally asked me out, it put me on cloud nine. We dated for a week, and things were great. Then he wanted to have sex and, of course, I was willing. But as soon as we had sex, he broke up with me and ignored me. I was devastated and my self-esteem was completely destroyed. Yet, I continued to seek out boys to "fulfill" me, only to repeat the cycle, over and over.

I also experienced situations where having sex wasn't my choice—situations that played a part in my life more than I would ever want to admit. One night, I was drunk at a party, and flirting with some guy who took me to the upstairs hallway of the house we were in. My brain, in that moment, was able to formulate some kind of sense despite my drunken stupor, and I told the boy, "No." But it was too late, and I was too trashed to defend myself, so he had sex with me anyway.

You would think after this happened that I would have learned. But I didn't. It happened again. I ended up drunk, in a bed with a boy, telling him to stop, and he didn't.

I buried the hurt and weight of these violations deep down inside of myself, not allowing it to enter my thoughts. I didn't show outwardly how badly I had been wounded; I kept it all hidden away, allowing the feelings of shame to slowly corrode my self-worth.

Despite being taken advantage of, I still thought sex would somehow be the answer to creating value within myself. But it never did. Sex only gave me temporary popularity and satisfaction on the outside, and a never-ending emptiness on the inside.

By the time I was a senior in high school, I had gotten most of the crazy random acts of promiscuity out of my system and settled into a "long-term" relationship. I dated the same guy for a year or so until I left for college. Then, within three days of breaking up with him, I found another guy at college whom I dated for two years.

Chapter One – Naked

However, even within these relationships, as I continued to have sex, hoping to be fulfilled with some kind of deeper value, I was repeatedly deflated. I couldn't satisfy that longing in my soul and couldn't increase my self-esteem. That made me think that I had to keep searching. I knew there was something that could make me feel treasured and give me the worth I didn't seem capable to give myself.

After college, I settled down and married my husband, Rob. But as I look back, I now realize that all my promiscuity created a lot of baggage. By that point in my life, I had learned the art of using sex to manipulate men. I would use it to get what I wanted, or withhold it when I was angry or frustrated. I also developed the ability to shut myself off from the experience. I could be having sex, and my mind could take me away to another place so I didn't have to engage emotionally.

As I began to realize this and work through figuring out how to relax and enjoy being intimate with the man I married, my low self-esteem continued to be a stumbling block for me. Rob is an amazing man who loves me so much; I have just put up so many walls to protect myself from what I experienced in high school that I can't let go a lot of the time. Being vulnerable is hard because of my past, even in the safe environment my husband wanted to create for me from the beginning.

A few years into my marriage, once I began my relationship with God, and explored and prayed about what sex was supposed to be, my perspective started to change. I realized that sex was never meant to be abused, or a substitute for real value or merit in my life. It was never to be thought of as gross, bad, or painful.

Instead, God taught me that sex was created as a reminder of the promise my husband and I made to Him when we got married.

God intended sex to be a beautiful bond between a married man and woman—a bond that is a place of vulnerability, trust, and love. A place to be naked and unashamed. A place that reveals to us the intimacy of God's relationship with us.

All this is a relatively new thought to me, and as I was working through trying to embrace this idea of what sex should be and the painfulness of the past memories that bring feelings of shame and guilt, I received some great advice from a sweet friend. She told me, "Praise God for the good and the bad, because you don't know which is which." I often look at all this garbage in my past and see nothing but bad. But God is now using that bad for good.

Romans 8:28 reads, "God uses all things for the good of those who love Him and have been called according to His purpose." My sweet husband says that God put all of this heartache and difficult memories in my life for a reason. These memories are a part of who I am and something I need to share so that you can see how God uses it for my good and His glory. And it might just be to encourage you.

> "Haven't you read," he replied, "that at the beginning the Creator 'made them male and female,' and said, 'For this reason a man will leave his father and mother and be united to his wife, and the two will become one flesh'? So they are no longer two, but one flesh. Therefore what God has joined together, let no one separate."
>
> Matthew 19:4-6

> "This is the verdict: Light has come into the world, but people loved darkness instead of light because their deeds were evil. Everyone who does evil hates the light, and will not come into the light for fear that their deeds will be exposed. But whoever lives by the truth comes into the light, so that it may be seen plainly that what they have done has been done in the sight of God.
>
> John 3:19-21

Drunk

I was so sick. I continued to vomit strawberry daiquiris long past the clock striking twelve. It was New Year's Eve, and I can't remember if it was my freshmen year or senior year of high school, but it doesn't matter, since it could have happened at either.

I began enjoying the sweet taste of liquor as a middle-schooler when I used to sneak cups of homemade wine coolers at my parents' Fourth of July parties. The wine coolers tasted delectable and yummy, just like the daiquiris did. And I found that the sweeter and more undetectable the taste of alcohol was, the more I indulged. It tasted harmless, but there were many hurts that could occur, and I was currently suffering one of them—one I was all too familiar with.

I lived most of my first three years of high school as a lie. You see, I wasn't that kid whose parents worried about sneaking out or drinking. I was the straight-A honor student. I was the "good

Nakedness

kid." I loved to do puzzles with my dad. I played with my Barbies way past the time it was cool to do so.

But I also snuck out and drank like a fish.

I never touched any "hard" drugs (and that's how I thought all of this "wasn't so bad" at the time), but loved all drinks that got me drunk quick. As a freshman in high school, I found a couple groups of older girls and senior boys to hang out with, which always provided a good party for consuming alcohol.

Weekends were filled with sleepovers at friends' houses whose parents either didn't care we were drinking or weren't around to stop us. My pattern was to create a lie to get where I needed to go, so I could drink and become somebody I wasn't.

It didn't matter where the drinking occurred—it even happened at church. I remember at a church lock-in one of the boys snuck in a bottle of vodka, and we got completely trashed. When we got caught, the boy who brought it took the fall for all of us. That was nice of him but, in hindsight, enabled me to continue binge drinking.

I'm fairly sure that I was addicted to alcohol, but not nearly as strongly as I was addicted to *who I became* when I drank. Alcohol made me *the fun girl*, who people wanted around. When I was sober, I was a goody-two-shoes, but with a couple drinks in me, I could be the *bad girl* and not worry about the consequences.

Drinking was also a way I thought I could quench the desire I felt deep inside—that same one I tried to fill with sex. Infused with alcohol, I thought I could be someone more, someone extraordinary. I wanted adventure and mystery, and this was my ticket to the ride. I thought for sure there was a better life for me somewhere at the bottom of the bottle. But the more I sought to fulfill what I thought was missing, the more lost I became.

I didn't know what I was supposed to be looking for. I hadn't a clue that the longing in my heart wasn't for simply an extraordinary life, but for something more. A *something* that would never be satisfied by anything I could consume.

Chapter One – Naked

One day, during my junior year, I was spending time at a boy's house with some friends. We were actually sober at the time, but the boys were up to mischief.

I was down in the basement when the boys came down the stairs with a twinkle in their eyes and an evil grin on their faces. They "playfully" grabbed me and attempted to tie me to a beam in the basement ceiling.

As my mind raced with fear, I instinctually began to fight and kick so I could get away fast.

I got out of the house and stood by my car, trying to come to grips with what had just happened.

As my two girlfriends who were with me came out of the house, laughing, and wondering why I was so upset, I began to unleash my frustration and anger on them. Looking back, I recognize that they were not the only reason I was mad. In that moment, my eyes began to open. I started to comprehend what a mess my life had become.

This was my wake-up call. I didn't know God at the time, so I wouldn't have given Him credit then, but because of what I know of Him now, I am sure He used this moment to help redirect me away from the dangerous and reckless life I had been living. I looked at who I had become and the path of destruction I was on, and did not like where I was headed.

But I couldn't stop everything completely. That would have displeased so many people, and I still desired to drink and be the "fun girl". I just thought I could do it in more controlled situations with good friends. The problem, though, was I began to see how many of my "friends" were not real friends. But to be honest, how could they have been real friends, when I wasn't real myself.

I had created this person that I wasn't—with a web of lies that I had orchestrated throughout my life. I was scared to let all that go; I knew of nothing else, and if I told the world the truth, I feared the consequences. So I didn't completely stop the drinking and the lies, but did begin to become aware of what I was doing.

Nakedness

During my senior year, the fear waned, and the maintenance of my fake persona became exhausting. So I determined two things. First, I was done with the lies and the drinking. My solution: I would run away from it all. My plan was to attend a college where I would not know anyone; I went seven hours away to a school in the middle of nowhere, where I was hoping that the life of lies I had been living could not follow.

Second was the anticipation that at college I would find the answer to the "something more" I had always longed for, because I now knew for sure that my deep desire could not be filled by alcohol. I was certain that with a change of environment, and a fresh start on life, I would be able to find the answers.

I went off to college, with visions of grandeur that I would be *real* and find the "something more" that was still missing. And it was throughout college that I began to see I couldn't outrun the lies, and that the life I was looking for, couldn't be found in anything I could consume.

As I delved into my past and first wrote down these stories, feelings of resentment and bitterness toward the people that hurt me came rushing to the surface. I had never forgiven them. Instead, I buried the hurt someplace deep, and had no idea it was still affecting me. I was wrong. They influence my self-esteem, my patience, and my temper.

Realizing this was one thing, but to forgive was not easy, especially when you have been mad at someone for so many years. But through God, all things are possible.

As I have explored, through prayer and Bible studies, what it means to have a relationship with God, I begin to learn to let go of all of this hurt and anger, because the only person it really hurts is me.

And when I think about the way that God has forgiven me of my

Chapter One – Naked

wrongs through His grace, I am reminded of how I need to let go and forgive those who hurt me so long ago.

Reflecting on these memories also reminds me of who I was then, and who I am now. It brings tears to my eyes and amazement to my heart that God has extended His grace, love, and forgiveness to me, an undeserving sinner. He has pulled me from the wreckage of the life I had created, and started me on a journey of hope toward the fulfilled life I had been seeking.

I am so thankful for it.

> **I CAN DO ALL THINGS THROUGH HIM WHO GIVES ME STRENGTH.**
>
> **PHILIPPIANS 4:13**

> **DO NOT GET DRUNK WITH WINE, FOR THAT IS DISSIPATION, BUT BE FILLED WITH THE SPIRIT.**
>
> **EPHESIANS 5:18**

Love

My first memory of my husband, Rob, was on a spring break trip to South Padre Island when we were sophomores in college. We had gone separately to the island, but he ended up sleeping at the place where I was staying on one of the nights. I wasn't happy with him, as he was "innocently" occupying one of the beds, and I ended up sleeping on the floor.

A few months later, when he was dating my roommate, I got to really know him for the first time. Seeing that he was actually a good guy, I made the decision to inform him that I thought he was "too good for my roommate." I had no romantic interest in him at the time, but of course, once we started to date, it certainly looked like I had.

Rob and I started really talking during the summer before our junior year—just socializing (maybe thinking about more, but nothing had happened yet). When everyone returned to school for the fall semester, I immediately got a call from my former roommate.

She began with, "I heard you've been sleeping with Rob!"

Chapter One – Naked

I immediately denied her accusation, because we weren't sleeping together.

Then, she accused me of kissing Rob, which I again denied, because we hadn't.

Finally, she said something that was true. "I heard you have been talking to him!"

"Yes, I've been talking to him, but that's all we've done."

After that, Rob and my innocent conversations did lead to kissing and dating, which only compounded the trouble. My ex-roommate and I were sorority sisters, and she still liked Rob, so we entered a very catty high school-like situation, where half of our sorority sided with her, and the other half with me.

The drama came to a head on what we called Bid Night, when all the fraternities accept their new members and have huge parties. Having just begun to "officially" date Rob, I didn't know many people in and around his fraternity, so I began the night by going to see him, and then left to go see my friends in the other fraternities—promising to come back.

I returned to Rob's fraternity late and did a walk through, but couldn't find him. A little disappointed, I went back to my car where I ran into a friend who wanted a ride home, so we both got into my car. At exactly that moment, I spotted Rob, in a field, talking to my ex-roommate. She was quite animated.

I don't do well with confrontation, so I put my car into reverse and looked behind me to back up. Out of nowhere, Rob flew across the hood of my car, Dukes of Hazzard–style, and said, "Take me with you!"

I shouted, "No!"

He opened the back door of my car, and got in anyway. I did the only thing I could; I drove away as my ex-roommate watched.

After that night, the drama subsided, and I settled into dating my picture-perfect dream guy. He was (and is) handsome and smart, with amazing integrity. My thinking was, since I saw him as perfect, surely he could make *me* perfect. So I began to rely on him to fill the deep longing I had always felt in my heart and soul.

I thought he was the answer to all my daydreams and was exactly what I had been searching for all my life. Therefore (in an unhealthy manner) I began to let his emotions define me. If Rob was happy with me, I felt worthy. But if he was upset with me, I thought of myself as dirt.

Rob and I dated our junior year, were engaged at the beginning of our senior year, and married the September after we graduated. It was a match made in heaven! Neither of us had a relationship with God at the time, but we both thought for sure that we were bound for "happily ever after." Complete bliss . . . the first couple of weeks. Then reality set in.

I am the perfect, oldest, golden child of *my* family. My husband is the perfect, oldest, golden child of *his* family. That created a mutual stubbornness—we were both very set in our ways. However, our "ways" were vastly divergent because of the two very different environments in which we were raised. That led to two very distinct views of what marriage was supposed to look like.

I was raised in a household where both parents worked. My dad was the "fun guy" and worked hard to be my best friend growing up. My mom worked hard to provide for our family and was the rule institutor and regulator. I wasn't close to her growing up, but learned a strong sense of independence and an "I am woman, hear me roar" mentality.

Overall, I felt like I had a great childhood and didn't lack anything. I never saw my parents fight or argue, which I later learned was because of their inability to communicate. They

Chapter One - Naked

secretly struggled until they filed for divorce the day I left for my honeymoon. Even after witnessing the demise of my parents' marriage, I remained a dreamer about what marriage was going to look like.

My head was filled with visions of Disney princesses being swept off their feet by their prince. Rob, on the other hand, wasn't in the sweeping-off-the-feet business and took no time in helping me realize what he thought marriage was supposed to look like.

Rob's household growing up had been quite different than mine. The first time I came home with Rob to meet his family, his mom made him French toast, buttered it, put syrup on it, and cut it into pieces for him (he was 21 at the time).

This is how he was raised—in a home where his mom stayed at home to care for the family and did all the cooking, cleaning, and laundry, while his dad went off to work and did not do household chores. His parents were great and their home was a place of warmth and love, but to me it was very "1950s," as I viewed it from the perspective of how I grew up. But *this* was Rob's picture of what marriage looked like, so of course, in his eyes, it was what ours would look like too.

Our first three years of marriage were challenging. Rob would flex his man card, I would flex my "woman, hear me roar" muscles, and our stubbornness often left us at odds. He also set the expectation that I was to be the cook and the cleaner, which I felt was incredibly unfair because we both worked, and in all honesty, I hated cleaning. So we simply "coexisted" for a while.

This was far from the vision I had of marriage, so I was not happy. Having never seen my parents argue left me ill-equipped to express what I was feeling. In my mind, Rob was supposed to be the answer to all my problems—to give me value, to satisfy the deep longing I had, and sweep me off my feet. But now, he no longer felt like the solution, which left me feeling like there must be something better, something that still might make me feel golden and perfect.

I started going out drinking with my friends, without Rob. I eventually ended up kissing two other men on different occasions. In my mind, I was just testing the water to see if this would make me feel better. It didn't.

There was never anything more than a kiss—which doesn't make it any less wrong—but in my case, made it possible for me to pick my head up and not feel all was lost.

Eventually, Rob and I had a big talk about our marriage and expectations. But even as we started to find some balance and growth, I kept my secret hidden deep within me—I was too afraid to tell it. It stayed buried a long time.

Years later, after I had begun to try to figure out what God's role was in my life, I felt it was important for me to reveal to Rob my deep dark secret of infidelity.

I argued with God and myself, and I put it off for a long time, but finally, I decided I could do it. With what felt like God's encouragement and thoughts of, *This is not a big deal, it was nine years ago*, I sat in the front seat of the car, and faced Rob while he was driving.

I smiled and said, with a small hint of excitement in my voice, as if I had good news to reveal, "I have something to tell you."

Quickly, I continued. I told Rob, "I kissed a guy back at the beginning of our marriage."

My husband retorted the word, "What!" with such venom in his voice I felt immediately deflated, and fear covered me in an oh-what-have-I-done way.

Chapter One - Naked

Rob pulled the car over and started grilling me for details, which I immediately began fudging and making less than they actually were. He eventually got out of the car and walked away.

Not knowing what to do now, I did the same. And as my foot hit the ground, my thoughts turned to regret and blame. I blamed God because I felt my obedience to Him seemingly made everything fall apart. I cried and asked God what He had gotten me into. But the only response I got was Rob telling me to get back into the car.

We drove home in complete silence.

The next week was shaky at best. I was really not sure whether we were going to make it or not. I held on to the only thing I could—my faith in God. Even though I had blamed Him for everything that had happened, I still trusted that He would get us through.

On Sunday, ten days after my confession, we went to church together, and the sermon happened to be about marriage. At the end of the sermon, the preacher invited all married couples to stand and renew their vows.

I sat, my heart pounding in my chest, unable to move, barely able to breathe—unable to look at Rob—unsure whether he would stand or not. And when he finally did, tears poured down my cheeks. I quickly stood too, and we renewed our vows through tears, praising God for this second chance.

Since then, Rob has forgiven me. I had the opportunity, several years later, to tell Rob the whole truth because, through prayer, Rob was able to create a safe environment for us to discuss all the details of who and where my infidelity occurred.

Rob and I have since become mentors for engaged couples, and it has blessed our own marriage immensely. Through this work, we have learned that, without God at the center of our marriage, we are bound to fail.

Nakedness

Rob is my best friend. He knows everything about me, and despite my thought that every day I couldn't love him more, I do. We have developed a completely open and honest relationship.

Don't get me wrong. Things are not always *complete bliss*—we still argue or get a little stubborn, and Rob is still not in the sweeping-off-the-feet business. We still often put unrealistic expectations on each other, and we don't always respond the way the other hopes.

But, despite all of the challenges, and all of our weaknesses, I know God has blessed me with Rob, and that Rob loves me in such a Godly way that there is nothing this side of heaven that can compare.

> "FOR THIS REASON A MAN WILL LEAVE HIS FATHER AND MOTHER AND BE UNITED TO HIS WIFE, AND THE TWO WILL BECOME ONE FLESH." THIS IS A PROFOUND MYSTERY - BUT I AM TALKING ABOUT CHRIST AND THE CHURCH. HOWEVER, EACH ONE OF YOU ALSO MUST LOVE HIS WIFE AS HE LOVES HIMSELF, AND THE WIFE MUST RESPECT HER HUSBAND.
>
> EPHESIANS 5:31-33

> SO, IF YOU THINK YOU ARE STANDING FIRM, BE CAREFUL THAT YOU DON'T FALL! NO TEMPTATION HAS SEIZED YOU EXCEPT WHAT IS COMMON TO MAN. AND GOD IS FAITHFUL; HE WILL NOT LET YOU BE TEMPTED BEYOND WHAT YOU CAN BEAR. BUT WHEN YOU ARE TEMPTED, HE WILL ALSO PROVIDE A WAY OUT SO THAT YOU CAN STAND UP UNDER IT.
>
> 1 CORINTHIANS 10:12,13

Fear

When I was thirteen, I went to see a movie that most would consider entertaining—*Ghostbusters*. I completely freaked when the arms came out of the chair. I immediately stood up and went to the restroom to hide, because I could no longer sit there. I can vividly remember that the monster-dog-things (from the film) chased me in my sleep for the next week.

This is just one example of many of how my mind found the things that were to be feared, and held on to them tightly. I can't tell you why—I don't know if it was because of my insecurities, my imagination, or because I knew there was always something to be afraid of, I just know I was often afraid.

Defined by Webster, fear is "an unpleasant often strong emotion caused by anticipation or awareness of danger." This unpleasant emotion was more than strong the first part of my life.

As a teenager, fear took a more tangible form when my best friend's mom died of Alzheimer's Disease. It was a scary thing to lose a parent at such a young age. I questioned if there was a

Nakedness

God—and if there was one, I wasn't sure I wanted to know Him after witnessing the hardships of my friend.

My anxieties continued to accumulate as I got older, but I always found new ways to hide or bury them, until I had my first baby. With the birth of my first child, fear found a new name. I was terrified! Terrified someone would steal my baby, terrified of my inability to protect this precious bundle, terrified of being a mother for the first time.

Sleep became a seldom occurrence. How could I keep my child safe if I was sleeping? I had to make sure nothing happened to her. And then, baby number two was on the way. Already sleep deprived and fearful, I had to find another way. I couldn't protect two babies and be functional all on my own. I had to find a way to face all the uncertainties so I could maneuver through life. I came upon two options: either medicate it or try some "faith."

I hadn't really given God much thought since my friend's mom had died. I had met with pastors as a requirement for my marriage and gone to church with my husband, but found myself more concerned with looking and acting as I was expected to, rather than seeking God.

A friend came to me just at the right time, with an invitation to a "Women of the Bible" book study, and I cautiously stepped in. Guarded and fearful, I attended the six-week study. It brought little reprieve to my anxieties, but I knew something was there—some kind of peace. Finally, something seemed to fit into and soothe that deep longing in my soul that I had never been able to fill, but it felt like there were answers I hadn't found yet, so I continued to seek.

Community Bible Study was what I found. I walked into a room full of ladies I didn't know, carrying a Bible I had never opened, and I was covered in fear. The ladies were less than warm and fuzzy, and the study was way over my head, but God was there, waiting for me and all of my trepidations.

He taught me that I shouldn't be anxious about anything, but in everything, by prayer and petition, with thanksgiving, present

Chapter One - Naked

my requests to Him (Philippians 4: 6). And I did. It was hard at first, and I thought it wasn't going to get any easier, but God didn't let me do it alone. He led me to a community within which I would grow.

The first time I stepped into a nondenominational church with my new faith, they sang the song "Healing Rain" by Michael W. Smith: "Healing rain. I'm not afraid to be washed in heaven's rain. Healing rain is falling down. Healing rain is falling down! I'm not afraid, I'm not afraid."

During "Healing Rain," God opened my heart and eyes to Him. I gave Him my fears and found a church home where God would begin a sweet relationship with me.

I still have apprehensions in my daily life, but I try to focus on a different definition of fear: "profound reverence and awe especially toward God," (Webster). This is the kind of fear that reminds me that I am not to be afraid of the something that goes bump in the night, but of a Wonderful Father who loves me with all His might.

Several years later, in Community Bible Study, I was asked to talk to the group about how I began to seek what it meant to have God in my life. As I reflected on my fears in preparation for that presentation–this description of what I see when I'm struggling between God and my fears or sins came to mind:

I see myself underwater in the dark; a single ray of light penetrates the darkness and a hand is extending into the water within that light. I struggle to reach the hand, but realize one of my hands is holding on to something very heavy and it is pulling me into the darkness, drowning me. I know if I can reach the hand offered in the light, it will pull me up to safety. I struggle to get there and I do. I reach the hand, but it can only pull me so far, because I won't release the heavy load I am holding.

Nakedness

As I get closer to the light, I can see a face above the water. But in order to get above the water and not drown in the darkness, I must let go of what I hold on to that is weighing me down. I fix my eyes on the glow of the face above the water and release the weight. As it sinks into the darkness, I am pulled into the light above the water where I look into the eyes of Jesus.

As long as I keep my eyes on His, I stay above water and in His light. It is when I look back at what I let go of, that I go back into the water and have to start all over again.

> THE LORD IS MY LIGHT AND MY SALVATION – WHOM SHALL I FEAR? THE LORD IS THE STRONGHOLD OF MY LIFE – OF WHOM SHALL I BE AFRAID?
>
> PSALM 27:1

> THERE IS NO FEAR IN LOVE. BUT PERFECT LOVE DRIVES OUT FEAR, BECAUSE FEAR HAS TO DO WITH PUNISHMENT. THE ONE WHO FEARS IS NOT MADE PERFECT IN LOVE.
>
> 1 JOHN 4:18

TWO *Steps*

A MAN'S STEPS ARE DIRECTED BY THE LORD. HOW THEN CAN ANYONE UNDERSTAND HIS OWN WAY.

PROVERBS 20:24

Secrets

My grandparents' house was a place of warmth and love, but also dark secrets. The first two I experienced firsthand and are what compose some of my favorite memories. The smell of their house that encompassed me as I walked through the front door always brought a smile to my face and immediately put me at ease. When I was lucky enough to sleep over, the routine was always the same—the best mac and cheese for dinner followed by cinnamon toast and chocolate milk on a TV tray so I could watch Dallas while I ate.

At bedtime, my grandma and I would lie in bed and talk forever, confessing and discussing all that was going on in my young life. The morning would begin with cereal at their tiny kitchen table, usually Frosted Shredded Wheat, and then a walk to the creek with Grandpa. With our trusted walking sticks, we would make it to the creek in no time, where we'd throw a few stones and then return home to Grandma, always creating a wildflower bouquet along the way.

Back at their house, we'd work in the garden harvesting a bountiful assortment of fruits and vegetables. It was so fun to pick and eat the fruits of our labor. The time there was precious, and beautiful memories were made.

Nakedness

I saw and experienced complete bliss, but as a child, I wouldn't have seen anything else. The only bad thing that I ever faced was that at some point, I would have the disappointment of leaving. I never saw my grandparents fight. I never saw anything that would lead me to believe this was anything but a loving home, loving toward me and within my grandparents' relationship.

But tucked away, hidden for no one to see, no one to know, buried underneath smiles and good times, were secrets—secrets of loneliness and sadness. My grandparents' relationship was far from bliss when no one else was around. They put their best foot forward when I was there, and I would never have known any differently had I not been told as an adult.

As I reflect on what I now know of my grandparents' secrets, it makes me look at my own life, and the warmth and love that I have always struggled to muster up to portray a "happy" facade to the world while the dark secrets are hidden away. I have often lived this illusion of bliss because experience has taught me to cover up all the problems, all the trials and tribulations, in order to keep everyone happy, keep myself in the right socially, and avoid ridicule or judgment. But when I hide away all the hardships, mistakes, and secrets, no one knows who I really am or what God can do through me.

This is why I believe God has called me to write. He is showing me that the secrets, brokenness, and imperfections have a purpose. When I try, like so many others, to cover up my past and my mistakes, so that no one will see my failures and inadequacies, I am hiding more than my faultiness. I'm hiding brokenness—brokenness that can be used to encourage and help others along in their journey. A brokenness that God has given me to show the world His light.

I now see that God is working through me, in this book, and in

Chapter Two - Steps

the chaos and mundane day-to-day activities of my life. I pray that you, too, will know that you are not alone in your brokenness. We are all broken, together.

> SEE TO IT THAT NO ONE TAKES YOU CAPTIVE THROUGH HOLLOW AND DECEPTIVE PHILOSOPHY, WHICH DEPENDS ON HUMAN TRADITION AND THE BASIC PRINCIPLES OF THIS WORLD RATHER THAN ON CHRIST.
>
> COLOSSIANS 2:8

> IF WE CLAIM TO BE WITHOUT SIN, WE DECEIVE OURSELVES AND THE TRUTH IS NOT IN US. IF WE CONFESS OUR SINS, HE IS FAITHFUL AND JUST AND WILL FORGIVE US OUR SINS AND PURIFY US FROM ALL UNRIGHTEOUSNESS. IF WE CLAIM WE HAVE NOT SINNED, WE MAKE HIM OUT TO BE A LIAR AND HIS WORD HAS NO PLACE IN OUR LIVES.
>
> 1 JOHN 1:8-10

Bliss

~~~~~~~~~~~

When we bought our house, we looked at the lot full of beautiful trees and were so thankful for this lovely piece of property. And we still are appreciative, even though my husband and I (with occasional forced assistance from my children), have spent entire days raking and bagging leaves!

We always end up exhausted and wondering how we missed the fact that all those beautiful, tall trees would lose their leaves in the fall, requiring a lot of hard work to clean up and take care of what God had blessed us with.

As I reflect on this task, two other very important things were brought to mind—things I've been blessed with, but have entered into with the same kind of "blind bliss."

The first is my marriage. As I mentioned in my chapter *Love*, my perception of marriage was completely different from my husband's during the early years of our marriage. Both of us had unrealistic expectations of the other and, eventually, it got hard—really hard. So we got to work.

With God's help, we figured out not only how to function as

Chapter Two - Steps

husband and wife, but also how to truly love one another. My husband and I are best friends, and abounding in love for each other, not because we're a match made in heaven (even though we are), but because of the amount of hard work and perseverance we put into our marriage.

The other important thing was when I started to get to know who Jesus was. All I heard about, as I began to pursue a relationship with God, was that I would be "saved" and going to heaven. People forgot to mention that it would change the very core of who I am. No one mentioned that suffering would be a big component. I never heard about how I would most likely be an outcast—even to some of my family and friends—because of my new-found love for God.

Loving Jesus amounts to a lot of hard work that I never knew I would have to do—like a continual swim upstream. It's a constant battle to choose God over myself, but I embrace this hard work here on Earth, because the work I do now is nothing compared to the awesomeness that awaits me in heaven.

> **DEAR FRIENDS, DO NOT BE SURPRISED AT THE FIERY ORDEAL THAT HAS COME ON YOU TO TEST YOU, AS THOUGH SOMETHING STRANGE WERE HAPPENING TO YOU. BUT REJOICE INASMUCH AS YOU PARTICIPATE IN THE SUFFERINGS OF CHRIST, SO THAT YOU MAY BE OVERJOYED WHEN HIS GLORY IS REVEALED.**
>
> **1 PETER 4:12,13**

> **LET PERSEVERANCE FINISH ITS WORK SO THAT YOU MAY BE MATURE AND COMPLETE, NOT LACKING ANYTHING.**
>
> **JAMES 1:4**

The Gate

Matthew 7:13-14 says: "Enter through the narrow gate. For wide is the gate and broad is the road that leads to destruction, and many enter through it. But small is the gate and narrow the road that leads to life, and only a few find it."

I find this verse profound as it presents me with two ways I can live my daily life: the narrow gate lifestyle is when I choose to stand for and represent Jesus, whereas when I choose to live life focused on the "world's way", it is reflective of the wide gate. I'll honestly say, I really don't know the percentage I do each, but I know I don't stand for Jesus enough.

I often embody the ways of the wide door because they are easy, but when I choose this easy way it decreases the opportunities to show the world what can be done by trusting God. It also doesn't show my kids a good way to deal with things when it gets tough. Letting them see how it may become even harder to do the right thing because I'm following what Jesus would do, sets the example of a life that is headed toward the narrow door.

Since the narrow door is obviously the tougher one to live for, I must be prepared to deal with even greater challenges and

Chapter Two - Steps

obstacles on top of those that I may already be facing. I can only equip myself so far, so I look to the one who can completely prepare me—Jesus.

Jesus epitomized a life lived for the narrow door every day, with more struggles and obstacles than I will ever encounter. He was capable, not only because He took the time to get away and pray, but also because He almost never faced any day without His friends. He was in continual community with the disciples. He always had a great support system of men and women who would help him out and, for the most part, looked out for Him.

What this looks like for me is getting in His Word and having time in prayer every day. This keeps His word running through my head like a ticker tape. It also means convening and surrounding myself with encouraging, reliable community that can help me persevere toward the narrow gate.

The wide gate is one that I am all too familiar with. I long to show the world what a life that is focused on the narrow gate looks like. And I challenge you, my friend, to come alongside me and live life for something greater than the easy and worldly way. Let's get equipped and represent Jesus together.

> **DO NOT LOVE THE WORLD OR ANYTHING IN THE WORLD. IF ANYONE LOVES THE WORLD, LOVE FOR THE FATHER IS NOT IN THEM.**
>
> **1 JOHN 2:15**

> **COMMIT YOUR WAY TO THE LORD; TRUST IN HIM AND HE WILL DO THIS: HE WILL MAKE YOUR RIGHTEOUS REWARD SHINE LIKE THE DAWN, YOUR VINDICATION LIKE THE NOON DAY SUN.**
>
> **PSALM 37:5,6**

THREE
It's Not About Me

Each of you should use whatever gift you have received to serve others, as faithful stewards of God's grace in its various forms. If anyone speaks, they should do so as one who speaks the very words of God. If anyone serves, they should do so with the strength God provides, so that in all things God may be praised through Jesus Christ. To him be the glory and the power for ever and ever. Amen.

1 Peter 4:10,11

Active

I embraced my sweet friend, and even though I was unsure of the cause of her tears, I knew she needed a hug. She composed herself, and looked at me with eyes that had been hurt before, but were desperately seeking hope—a hope that I had unknowingly offered by the questions I had asked. This lady, who had blessed so many through her work with the homeless, who had taught me so much about serving others, and what an active faith in Jesus actually looks like, was looking to me for hope.

Until that moment, I had not grasped the effect our Bible Study Group was having on her and her ministry. We came, when it was convenient for us, cooked food, and brought extra food for later in the week, but I always approached "serving the homeless" as a scheduled activity or planned event, as in, "We have a football game Saturday," or, "We have piano lessons on Tuesday." It was nothing more than another thing to do.

I probably would have continued this ministry with that mindset if my heart hadn't been stirred beyond this thought—helping me realize that my faith is meant to be more than just "I believe."

Nakedness

James 2:14-17 reads:

> What good is it, my brothers and sisters, if someone claims to have faith but has no deeds? Can such faith save them? Suppose a brother or a sister is without clothes and daily food. If one of you says to them, "Go in peace; keep warm and well fed," but does nothing about their physical needs, what good is it? In the same way, faith by itself, if it is not accompanied by action, is dead.

My faith was never meant to be just a proclamation of belief. Once I have stood up and said, "I love Jesus," my life should reflect that in every way. And this is not out of obligation, but realization of what faith stands for—an outward expression of the love, trust, and hope I have in Jesus.

This life of living active faith calls me to love others, give encouragement, and follow God's plan, even when it is inconvenient and uncomfortable. It's more than going through the motions of doing what I think God wants me to do—it's about embracing faith in a much more tangible way. This comes from the depths of my soul, and from the Spirit that a relationship with God has stirred within me.

Helping my friend feed the homeless should not be another thing on my "to do" list. It's not just another activity to participate in. It's a commitment to come beside this woman and walk with her on this journey. It's an opportunity to create and grow deeper relationships. It's the chance to give hope to the hopeless and live an active and living faith that proclaims God's glory.

Chapter Three - It's Not About Me

AS THE BODY WITHOUT THE SPIRIT IS DEAD, SO FAITH WITHOUT DEEDS IS DEAD.

JAMES 2:26

FOR THE WORD OF GOD IS ALIVE AND ACTIVE. SHARPER THAN ANY DOUBLE-EDGED SWORD, IT PENETRATES EVEN TO DIVIDING SOUL AND SPIRIT, JOINTS AND MARROW; IT JUDGES THE THOUGHTS AND ATTITUDES OF THE HEART.

HEBREWS 4:12

Clarity

My wonderful husband travels weekly for his job. One Friday, he was returning home, tired, worn down, and feeling sick. And I knew a clean house would be a great way to welcome him home. So I cleaned the house as if I was cleaning for Jesus. This means that I *tried* to focus on doing this service for the Lord, because I really do not like to clean.

When my exhausted, run-down husband walked through the door, he didn't notice what I had done. He could only see the things that *weren't* done, and in his weary state, that's what he commented on.

I can write this with understanding and compassion now, but I possessed neither of those feelings at the time. I had my panties in all kinds of bunches! Which led me to do the only thing I could—I went for a walk to get some clarity from the Lord.

I started running to get out all my frustration, and when I couldn't fume or run anymore, I began walking. That is when I noticed how amazing the sky was. It was the crispest, clearest blue I had ever seen. Everything seemed to "pop" against it. It served as an

Chapter Three – It's Not About Me

amazing contrast to my frustration. It is really hard to describe the sight—almost like walking in a virtual world. It was this clarity, exemplified in my environment, that led me to understand how unclear my thinking had been only moments earlier.

My hurt feelings had made me so frustrated, I couldn't see straight and I could only hear one thing—me—my voice telling me how right I was. My vision was completely distorted, but God had the perfect clarifying solution: stop listening to myself, and start listening to Jesus. As I opened my Bible later that evening, I read Colossians 2:6,7.

> Just as you received Christ Jesus as Lord, continue to live in Him, rooted and built up in Him, strengthened in the faith as you were taught, overflowing with thankfulness.

Through this verse Jesus was telling me where I needed to focus. By having an upward focus in my daily life, I am truly humble, and the empty vessel Jesus needs me to be—it's not about serving anyone but Him. Life is no longer about *me*, or the people's actions around me; it's about Jesus and His love of those people.

This verse also said I was to be "overflowing with thankfulness," thankful for the abundant blessings in my life. This reminded me that when I am appreciative for all that God has given me, it brings great clarity to my life, and helps me remember what is truly important.

Then I read Colossians 3:23. "Whatever you do, work at it with all your heart, as working for the Lord, not for men," which revealed to me that I had not done the mundane task of cleaning the house with all my heart for *Jesus*. If I had been, I wouldn't need the approval and pat on the back from my *husband*. By searching for earthly approval, I was acting as though Jesus' approval wasn't enough, and putting an expectation on my husband that he couldn't meet at that moment.

Too often, blind frustration is my knee-jerk reaction, but I pray that by putting these verses in my heart, I will more often react in a way that shows I have a mind that is as clear as the bright blue sky on that day.

Nakedness

How can you say to your brother, "Let me take the speck out of your eye," when all the time there is a plank in your own eye? You hypocrite, first take the plank out of your own eye, and then you will see clearly to remove the speck from your brother's eye.

Matthew 7:4,5

Trust in the Lord with all your heart and do not lean on your own understanding; in all your ways submit to Him and He will make your paths straight.

Proverbs 3:5-6

Perception

There is an old Portuguese story that tells of an old man who has a series of, what would seem to be, good and bad things happen to him. As the villagers react to each event, describing it as good or bad, the old man consistently restates the circumstance, and that it is just that, a situation, neither good nor bad; it just is. At the end of the tale he says, "No one is wise enough to know if it is a blessing or a curse. Only God knows."

I read this tale a long time ago and subconsciously had begun to apply it to my life. Now I feel the need to consciously make the effort to look at things that happen in my life as neither good, nor bad, but essentially what God has planned for that moment. This can be very challenging at times.

There was a day that I was supposed to go shopping the night before a trip but it got too hectic, so it didn't happen. I could have been agitated and frustrated, but counted it as God's will and moved on. The next morning my refrigerator wasn't working and I had to throw most of the food out. I thanked God for preventing my shopping trip the night before.

In this type of situation I am much more able to sit back and say, "God has a plan and I don't know it, but He has all things

Nakedness

happening for a reason." My problems with God's plan arise when I'm emotionally invested. I take the result of the situation personally, making it about me, even though it's not. In those instances I can't see past me—my hurt, my feelings, my head telling me a hundred things. I can't see how God is using me and growing me in that moment, and I can't see how it really is about Him—not me!

In the Bible, Daniel knew from the beginning that it wasn't about him. It was about God and His Sovereignty. Even as Daniel was being taken prisoner by the Babylonians, he could have thought it was a bad deal, but he didn't, because he knew God was in control. He had complete trust in God, who just handed his entire nation over to a pagan empire.

All the way to the end of his captivity, Daniel held on to God's plan with both hands. When a decree was sent out that only the king should be prayed to, what did Daniel do? He went back to his house and prayed to God, "as he had always done." Didn't flinch, didn't panic, didn't waver. He trusted God because he knew God was in control.

I am being constantly reminded about how much I am *not* in control. Even with this knowledge, I still fight for it for some strange reason. Every detail, no matter how small, is all a part of a greater plan. It is changing my perspective with the challenges and adventures I encounter in life, both the easy to give to God and the emotional (it's not about me!). It has also redefined the term "everything happens for a reason" to "everything happens for God's reasons."

Even though I still am constantly working on not perceiving situations as good or bad, I am now consciously thinking that no matter what I think it is, it is exactly as God wants it to be at that moment.

Chapter Three - It's Not About Me

Praise be to the Name of God for ever and ever; wisdom and power are His. He changes times and seasons; He sets up kings and deposes them. He gives wisdom to the wise and knowledge to the discerning. He reveals deep and hidden things; He knows what lies in darkness and light dwells with Him.

Daniel 2:20-22

Now I, [Insert name], praise and exalt and glorify the King of Heaven, because everything He does is right and all His ways are just. And those who walk in pride, He is able to humble.

Daniel 4:37

FOUR
Encouragement

But encourage one another daily, as long as it is called "Today," so that none of you may be hardened by sin's deceitfulness. We have come to share in Christ, if indeed we hold our original conviction firmly to the very end.

Hebrews 3:13,14

Atta Girl!

I was running along our hike-and-bike trail in town, and as I was finishing my run I caught up to and passed another woman who was running. Now, I'm not a marathoner, or even a "runner," so for me to pass someone else who is running is rare. But as I passed her, I felt God nudge me to encourage her.

I don't know if she was at the end of a ten-mile run, at the beginning of a long run, or, like me, struggling to finish a short one-mile run, but God was calling me to encourage her—to help her along to know she wasn't going to finish alone.

But I couldn't do it. I was apprehensive of speaking to this stranger, and I didn't even tell her, "Good job". This made me reflect, as I walked around the rest of the trail, on how as a child of God it's important for me to be an encourager *and* encouraged.

God has put me in different people's paths and different people in my path to help each other out along the way. Whether it's relatability, personality, or just to make me smile, I have been blessed with a wonderful group of people who keep me going.

Some have more Bible knowledge and wisdom than I feel I could ever have, others are new in their faith and others have no faith.

Nakedness

Each one plays a unique role and touches my life in the special way that God has designed for them.

This encouragement God has blessed me with is something I try to pass along to others. I find my sweet friends are easier to encourage than strangers and those that are more knowledgable or self sufficient than I am. But why?

We all need encouragement. No matter how put together or unfamiliar a person may be, we all need someone to keep us going when it's tough or to laugh with us when it's fun. That's why God has put that little urge on all of our hearts to encourage a stranger or friend, like He did mine.

I didn't see that lady again, but I saw another lady who I had seen walking earlier, and she was now running. I shouted, "Good job!" and, "Keep going!" her way, and my heart was immediately filled with great joy, letting me know that God was pleased and glorified by my willingness to encourage another along the path of life.

As I close this thought I say to you, even if we have never met: Keep going my friend, sister, or brother! God has told me to cheer for you and hold your hand through this journey. Remember, you can do all things through Christ who gives you strength. (Philippians 4:13).

> THEREFORE ENCOURAGE ONE ANOTHER AND BUILD EACH OTHER UP, JUST AS IN FACT YOU ARE DOING.
>
> 1 THESSALONIANS 5:11

> MAY OUR LORD JESUS CHRIST HIMSELF AND GOD OUR FATHER, WHO LOVED US AND BY HIS GRACE GAVE US ETERNAL ENCOURAGEMENT AND GOOD HOPE, ENCOURAGE YOUR HEARTS AND STRENGTHEN YOU IN EVERY GOOD DEED AND WORD.
>
> 2 THESSALONIANS 2:16-17

FIVE
Object

"For I know the plans I have for you," declares the Lord, "plans to prosper you and not to harm you, plans to give you hope and a future"

Jeremiah 29:11

Captive

I love my family, friends, food, my bed and hot showers. Jesus is on the list too—but if you ask me, "What is the object of your love?" even though I might answer Jesus, I can honestly tell you there are times my actions in life would indicate that *other* things take precedence.

I began thinking about this when my Community Bible Study of Colossians gave a list of attributes that should be happening in my life as I pursue a relationship with Jesus. It said, "He must become the focus of our attention, the object of our love, and the purpose for our life. There should be order in our lives, strength in our faith, and gratitude in our hearts." The study followed this list with the question, "Which [of the things on the previous list] do you especially feel lacking in or yearn for more of?"

As I reviewed the list, I felt, "Jesus as the object of my love," was what I lacked and yearned for most. Through prayer, Jesus led me to understand that when I love Him the most, He becomes the source and place that all my love comes from. I wondered why, of all the things listed that my heart felt this one was where I was lacking. I found the answer in the memory verse for that study: "See to it that no one takes you captive through hollow and deceptive philosophy, which depends on human tradition

Nakedness

and the basic principles of this world rather than on Christ." (Colossians 2:8).

If you compare my time spent in the Bible and in prayer versus my time in the "world," it would show that I behold the world much more than Jesus. This captivation with the world and lack of eagerness to hunt for the precious treasure that is found in the Bible prevents me to love Jesus and get to know Him. And if I don't know Him, I can't truly understand the depth of His love for me.

With Jesus in His rightful place as the "object of my love," He can turn my love into the love of the Bible—the love-your-enemies love and love-your-neighbor-as-yourself love, the unselfish and non-manipulative love. The 1 Corinthians 13 love. The love that knows no end and can reach to the depth of your soul and every soul you meet.

That is what I am yearning for! For Jesus to be such the object of my love, that every interaction is met with His grace and love rather than my shortcomings.

As I contemplated the "object of my love" phrase, God reminded me that I am the object of His love and what that love looks like: He loved me enough to create me, even though He knew I would cause Him pain and fail Him continuously.

God loved me enough to send Jesus to this destructive world of sin, where He was tempted beyond anything I could imagine and still remained sinless. Jesus suffered and died a cursed death on the cross, where he took the wrath of God, that was to be poured out on me because of my sin, all upon Himself and gave me His righteousness. He died for me and then rose from the dead so that He could stand and intercede for me to the Father daily.

This immeasurable love is even more amazing because God does not need me. I do nothing to complete Him or offer Him something He can't have or create Himself—He just loves me.

I am the object of His love.

Chapter Five - Object

> For I am convinced that neither death nor life, neither angels nor demons, neither the present nor the future, nor any powers, neither height nor depth, nor anything else in all creation, will be able to separate us from the love of God that is in Christ Jesus our Lord.
>
> Romans 8:38-39

> Love is patient, love is kind. It does not envy, it does not boast, it is not proud. It does not dishonor others, it is not self-seeking, it is not easily angered, it keeps no record of wrongs. Love does not delight in evil but rejoices with the truth. It always protects, always trusts, always hopes, always perseveres. And now these three remain: faith, hope and love. But the greatest of these is love.
>
> 1 Corinthians 13:4-7, 13

Talents

There came a day when I had had enough with the irresponsibility of my children. Their toys were everywhere, and they weren't very good at picking up after themselves, which left the house a mess. I know I'm to blame for a lot of this because I find it easier, faster, and less frustrating to just do it myself, but this method of cleanup wears me thin. So I introduced one of Jesus's great parables, and it ended up teaching us all a lesson.

Matthew 25:14-30 tells of a man who was going on a journey. Before he left, he called his servants to him and gave them each a bit of his property: "To one he gave five talents of money, to another, two talents, and to another, one talent, each according to his ability." (v.15). Then the man left and each man took his talents and did what he knew best with them. The men with five and two talents found ways to multiply their gifts. The man with one was scared of losing it so he dug a hole and buried it.

When the master returned he asked each man what he had done with what he was given. The two who multiplied their gifts he's pleased with and invites them to more responsibility. The man who has done nothing but hide his talent gets it taken away and is thrown in jail.

Chapter Five - Object

The parable concludes with verse 29: "For everyone who has will be given more, and he will have an abundance. Whoever does not have, even what he has will be taken from him," which I found confusing until I read my Bible commentary on the verse, which made it clear. It says, "Being ready for Christ's coming involves more than playing it safe and doing little or nothing. It demands the kind of service that produces results!"

After explaining this story to my children, they were instructed to choose their five favorite toys. The rest were going to be put away until they showed they could be responsible for their stuff—manage their talents. When they proved responsible for what they had, then they could come and select one toy to increase their talents. We will continue on this way for however long it takes to get toys back, but if we regress and get careless, I'll take more away, motivating them to manage their talents well.

A day after the great toy takeaway, the Lord, through prayer, inquired of me: "How are you managing the abilities and gifts I have given you?" Hmmm.

On this particular day I was overwhelmed and my house was a mess and the chaos of life was swallowing up me and my talents. It really made me stop and contemplate the way I "bury" my talents—not in the dirt but in my busy life.

God has blessed me abundantly, equipped me with many abilities and gifts, and given me directions on what to do with those talents. Unfortunately, I'm not always multiplying and embracing the importance of using them. When I'm communing with God, whether at church, Bible study, or in the morning, I'm ready! I grab my talents and set out to multiply.

My stumble occurs as soon as I walk out the door—life hits me from the front, and the back, then the left and the right. Before I know it, my talents are buried and so is my zest. I can't multiply what I can't find. I can't accomplish a purpose I can't see.

These are the days God opens my eyes to the ways I try to fit Jesus into my busy life rather than work my busy life around Jesus. He reminds me that He has given "each according to his ability." If I'm not making the most of what God has given me, it's not because He has given me too much, it is because I have mismanaged it by not prayerfully considering what God wanted me to do with it.

As my children learn to manage their talents, I, too, am looking at the blessings, talents, and purpose God has bestowed upon me. I am, through prayer, exploring new ways to keep these things unburied in the midst of life's chaos.

> We have different gifts, according to the grace given to each of us. If your gift is prophesying, then prophesy in accordance with your faith; if it is serving, then serve; if it is teaching, then teach; if it is to encourage, then give encouragement; if it is giving, then give generously; if it is to lead, do it diligently; if it is to show mercy, do it cheerfully.
>
> Romans 12:6

> There are different kinds of gifts, but the same Spirit distributes them. There are different kinds of service, but the same Lord. There are different kinds of working, but in all of them and in everyone it is the same God at work.
>
> I Corinthians 12:4-6

Pause

On Easter weekend, we grieve the death of Jesus and celebrate His rising from the grave. We are blessed to know the outcome between Friday and Sunday, but can you imagine having been one of the disciples on Saturday?

They watched their friend, the Messiah, and the source of hope, be rejected and beaten, mocked and persecuted, flogged and killed. Jesus had told them that it would all happen this way, and that He would rise again, but on Saturday there was a pause.

Not only did these friends and followers grieve, but they also probably had a good portion of doubt and hopelessness. They had followed Jesus, forsaking everything they had ever known, and now, in this moment, He was gone. God made them wait.

Think of the impact of this wait! It instilled an even greater value to their journey for Jesus. During this pause, there was an opportunity to reflect on all they had seen and heard.

Then, He came back, and the magnitude of His return was heightened by the delay of it.

In this day, where waiting is becoming a thing of the past, God still makes us wait from time to time. I can immediately text or

Nakedness

email, and the TV promises instant gratification for almost anything, yet in daily life, I wait for answers, for miracles, and for red lights.

Here's the amazing thing: each small and grand thing I wait for is an opportunity to add value to the end result. The pause is a chance for me to prepare my heart for whatever will happen next—to take this second to focus on God. I have to be intentional in that moment to make the most of it. Whether it's a chance for me to catch up and take a breath, or to truly feel the impact of what is about to or has happened, I need to live that pause. When I don't, I just might miss what God needs me to discover.

A great example of this is the huge pause that all of God's creation is in right now. We are waiting for Jesus to return—again! Jesus promised, before He ascended to heaven, that He would return one day to bring an end to tears and pain, to establish a new heaven and a new earth.

As I wait for this second coming, what am I doing to live out this pause?

Am I clinging to Him, longing for His presence? Am I strengthening my relationship with Him so I know what to look for upon His return?

We have the knowledge that He is going to come again, but like the disciples, we don't know when. But we do know how. Revelation 19:11-16 describes it like this:

> I saw heaven standing open and there before me was a white horse, whose rider is called Faithful and True. With justice he judges and wages war. His eyes are like blazing fire, and on his head are many crowns. He has a name written on him that no one knows but he himself. He is dressed in a robe dipped in blood, and his name is the Word of God. The armies of heaven were following him, riding on white horses and dressed in fine linen, white and clean. Coming out of his mouth

Chapter Five - Object

is a sharp sword with which to strike down the nations. 'He will rule them with an iron scepter.' He treads the winepress of the fury of the wrath of God Almighty. On his robe and on his thigh he has this name written: KING OF KINGS AND LORD OF LORDS.

That's motivation for me to go out and make the most of every time I have to wait. Because what I do in the pauses of life is sometimes what makes the greatest and most glorifying impact for God.

> For you were once darkness, but now you are light in the Lord. Live as children of light (for the fruit of the light consists in all goodness, righteousness and truth) and find out what pleases the Lord.
>
> Ephesians 5:8-10

> So that you may live a life worthy of the Lord and please him in every way: bearing fruit in every good work, growing in the knowledge of God, being strengthened with all power according to his glorious might so that you may have great endurance and patience.
>
> Colossians 1:10-11

SIX
Chasing

Where can I go from Your Spirit? Or where can I flee from your presence? If I ascend into heaven, You are there; if I make my bed in hell, behold, You are there. If I take the wings of the morning and dwell in the uttermost parts of the sea. Even there Your hand shall lead me, And your right hand shall hold me.

Psalm 139:7-10

Stop, Pray, and Follow

Summer is always an adventure for my family. Usually the first week is quite busy, but eventually our schedule begins to feel like summer and I am ready for a chill day. At which point I think my children are too—but I'm usually wrong.

There was one particular day that my children were far from chilling. By midmorning they were all picking and yelling at each other. By one o'clock I sent them all to their rooms for some quiet time—I needed quiet time. By the time my husband came home I was in tears!

I was so frustrated with my children. I was so spent and saddened by the fact that all I did the entire day was nag, yell, and be agitated with these precious gifts from God. I found most of the day, I had been caught up with what my kids were not doing right, I became pained inside by the fact that they were not obeying and acting as "proper" children should. Or maybe that's the problem—they were behaving like children should.

The lack of structure in the summer is challenging for them and for me, it feels like a constant time in the trenches and chaos, but God used this time to give me clarity by teaching me to shift my perspective.

Through the disorder, I was reminded how much I need the routine also. Without it, I tend to get worldly tunnel vision. This change in perspective from God to my earthly desires makes everything feel and seem more difficult and never ending. I feel like my initial reaction is as if I'm stuck in the mud, sinking fast. I start going on my reactions to the frustration and pain rather than follow an easy three-step rule: stop, pray, and follow Jesus.

When I take a breath in and exhale with a "Help me, Jesus!" it gives Him time to take the lead so I know where to go and what to say. In this moment, I can refocus on Him, gaining a different perspective. If I'm looking up I can see His hand extended to me to pull me out of where I'm stuck.

He then reminds me that there is so much more than this—that this moment with my children is a gift and has a purpose bigger than me, giving me hope to embrace this as my opportunity to show my kids Jesus. By surrendering to God my time, life, decisions and everything, I gain His perspective and am empowered by Him to do exactly what He would do. Why would I want to do it any other way?

> A SOFT ANSWER TURNS AWAY WRATH, BUT A HARSH WORD STIRS UP ANGER.
>
> PROVERBS 15:1

> I LOVE YOU, O LORD, MY STRENGTH. THE LORD IS MY ROCK, MY FORTRESS AND MY DELIVERER; MY GOD IS MY ROCK, IN WHOM I TAKE REFUGE. HE IS MY SHIELD AND THE HORN OF MY SALVATION, MY STRONGHOLD.
>
> PSALM 18:1,2

Pursuit

I took on the adventure of taking my four children to the mall. Despite not being a mall person and having no passion for shopping, I had things to return and kids that needed out of the house. As we perused and window-shopped, we stumbled upon the Apple Store.

Have you ever been in the Apple Store? It's way fun for kids and adults. They have tables full of computers, iPods, iPads, and iPhones—all for you to play with and figure out how you will be completely unable to live without this device. It's genius.

At one point I had all four of my kids, each on their own iPad, playing Angry Birds. But as I stood and watched my children play the game, I found myself eyeing and eventually wanting and justifying the need for an iPhone. I don't need an iPhone, but the temptation in that store was heightening my needs for the things of this world and challenging my pursuit of God.

The term "Pursuing God" was on my mind as I had been reading Proverbs. Proverbs is such an interesting book of the Bible. It clearly lays out God's dos and don'ts in a black-and-white format.

I follow Jesus, I love Jesus, I want to glorify Him, but "pursuit" was

Nakedness

never one of the words I grasped on to or would use to describe my journey to Jesus. I love the word though. It adds urgency and passion to the way I look to follow Jesus.

As I read through the book of Proverbs in the Bible, I am overwhelmed and convicted about how often I am pursuing the world—especially when I become overly concerned about missing out on something here. I get so consumed about what I need or don't have, that my mind becomes focused on stuff and not Jesus.

This is the mentality that can make me really miss out on something amazing, something so much greater than me, something I need so much more than an iPhone!

So what should the pursuit of God look like in my life, and what effect does it have? In Deuteronomy 6:6-8, it says to put the Lord's commands "upon your hearts. Impress them on your children. Talk about them when you walk along the road, when you lie down and when you get up. Tie them as symbols on your hands and bind them on your foreheads. Write them on the door frames of your houses and on your gates."

I'm so moved just to type these verses. Pursuing God is constant and active—it shouldn't be determined by my mood or circumstances, or who I'm with or where I am—it's simply me living on mission for God all the time.

Every time I choose to pursue the world instead of Jesus, there's a negative effect on my relationship with Him. He has blessed me in the perfect amount of everything so that I can bless others and grow in Him. It's when I pursue other things that I am letting Jesus know that what He has given me is not enough—you, Jesus, are not enough. How can I tell my God and Creator who laid down His life for me that "it's not enough"? But that's exactly what I am doing.

Now when I am in pursuit of Jesus, the effect is my growing relationship with Him and all the amazing bonuses that go with it. The rewards are in heaven and even though I cannot wrap my mind around the shortness of this life and the eternity of eter-

Chapter Six - Chasing

nity (which creates part of my struggle with pursuing God all the time), I can only pray that God will change my heart and my perspective so my pursuit of Him will look like His unrelenting, loving, constant pursuit of me.

> But you, man of God, flee from all this, and pursue righteousness, godliness, faith, love, endurance, and gentleness. Fight the good fight of the faith. Take hold of the eternal life to which you were called when you made your good confession in the presence of many witnesses.
>
> 1 Timothy 6:11, 12

> This is what the LORD, the God of Israel, says; "I anointed you king over Israel, and I delivered you from the hand of Saul. I gave your master's house to you, and your master's wives into your arms. I gave you the house of Israel and Judah. And if all this had been too little, I would have given you even more."
>
> 2 Samuel 12:7b, 8

Be Still

I was having one of those days filled with lots of battles. My younger two kids were whining and arguing, and the older two were wild and persnickety with each other and everybody else. By five o'clock, it was time to go to the pool.

I was tired and worn down attempting to do it all in my own strength. The pool, I hoped, would be a break from the nitpicking and fighting. After arriving at the pool, everyone dispersed to do their own thing. I usually just hang out in the shallow end with one eye on each my four-year-olds, and this time I grabbed my goggles as I headed there.

I strapped my goggles in place, jumped in, and put my head under the water only to be taken aback by the most peaceful scene that laid before me. Despite all the people in the water and around me, the direction I looked was empty of all except water and the sunlight streaming into it. As peaceful as what my eyes perceived, the real peace came in how it was completely silent and still under the water. This picturesque moment brought me back to the feet of God.

And then He blessed me even more by placing my younger children into the picture. This may not sound like a blessing, but it

Chapter Six - Chasing

was. As I watched my children in this underwater silent world, I could truly see them. During the day because of chaos and their whining, I may look at them, but see them through tired, weary eyes.

Here, there was nothing to take away from their precious faces and the obvious joy that exudes from their souls. Here I saw how big they're getting as well as their innocence. Here God gave me clarity and indescribable peace.

I struggle to get clarity and peace all the time, and I know it is a result of the life I live— technologically infused and overbooked. There's barely room for me to breathe much less get quiet with God.

The other day I was reflecting on Paul—the amazing Paul who wrote the majority of the New Testament. I thought about his travels and ministry—he was a busy man. He had to be "on" all the time to talk and debate and share the Gospel. He also had to work to support himself in the towns he traveled to, but despite how chaotic his life may have seemed, He valued his time with the Lord.

Throughout the New Testament, Paul tells us how he was constantly praying (Ephesians 1:15, Colossians 1:9, 2 Thessalonians 1:11) and encouraging those he's writing to, to pray all the time (Ephesians 6:18, Colossians 4:2, 1 Thessalonians 5:17). He took the time to get quiet and have ongoing conversations with the Lord, which helped him receive God's direction and calm.

Quiet time is so important to my relationship with Jesus. This is where He renews and refreshes me; hears my struggles. I try to get up and get with God before all else in the morning. Giving the Lord this time is truly a peaceful time and starts my day with my heart and head in the right place.

Nakedness

I find, though, that getting quiet isn't a "once a day" type of thing. By 11am, if I haven't tried to seek God in prayer again, I'm struggling! And by three o'clock, it's time for Mommy to have a time out and find someplace to be still with God so I can make it to the end of the day. It doesn't happen very often though, and that's when clarity and peace are replaced with fuzzy brain and chaos. I can't "see" my kids, much less God in this state.

One faithful thing Jesus does is meet me here—even when I don't get quiet. He meets me under water, or in a song, or with the warm breeze, or through a friend. He is always right there, ready for me to take just a moment to get quiet and just be still and know He is God, so he can refresh me and bless me and give me His peace.

> BE STILL AND KNOW I AM GOD; I WILL BE EXALTED AMONG THE NATIONS, I WILL BE EXALTED IN THE EARTH.
>
> PSALM 46:10

> GOD IS OUR REFUGE AND OUR STRENGTH, AN EVER-PRESENT HELP IN TROUBLE.
>
> PSALM 46:1

SEVEN
Instructions

All Scripture is God-breathed and is useful for teaching, rebuking, correcting and training in righteousness, so that the servant of God may be thoroughly equipped for every good work.

2 Timothy 3:16,17

Humble Pie

On one of our family vacations we decided to unplug ourselves from the world. It was wonderful. But as we arrived at our little, rented townhouse, I immediately started ticking off what was wrong with the place. Apparently, I had built up a little righteousness, judgmental jadedness over the summer, because I was looking down my nose at "all" these things that were not up to my standard.

The morning after our arrival, hammering due to the construction of a new unit right next door woke me up. This did not improve my attitude. As I sat and had my "quiet time" with God, I was continually distracted by my thoughts about how I was going to write a not-so-pleasant review about this place when we left—keep in mind we hadn't been there for 24 hours yet. I seriously needed some humble pie. And leave it to the Lord to serve it up in His own special way.

As I was getting ready for the day, my kids were swimming in the community pool, which was right out our backdoor, when all of a sudden my oldest runs into our place to inform me that my four-year-old son pooped in the pool. Out I go to use towels and my hands to fish poop out of the public, community pool.

I then humbly called the management—not to let them know why I am so above all these things that I have found wrong with their place, but to inform them that my son pooped in the pool and they need to come shock it. Humble pie!

As I reflected on this whole scenario, I realized that when I am in this "high and mighty" mindset, I have no need for God. God reminded me in Matthew 9:13b: "for I have not come to call the righteous, but the sinners." I can't hear or see my own mistakes and wrongs because I have my self-pretentious blinders on. Jesus has come for the sinners. I'm a sinner and I need to continuously humble myself and remember that the only way I'm righteous is through Jesus.

When I find myself in this self-righteous state, one of the things I seem to be lacking is my "awe" of God. My computer dictionary defines awe as: "a feeling of reverential respect mixed with fear or wonder." When was the last time I stood in reverential respect mixed with fear and wonder toward my Heavenly Father, Almighty Creator of me and everything else?

To begin my search for my awe of God I went to Scripture, where there is no shortage of passages that discuss the awe of God. The one God brought me to, though, tells one reason why He is worthy of my awe. Daniel 4:34b -35: "For His dominion is an everlasting dominion, and His kingdom endures from generation to generation. All the inhabitants of the earth are accounted as nothing, But He does according to His will in the host of heaven and among the inhabitants of earth; And no one can ward off His hand or say to Him, 'What have You done?'"

This is stated by the pagan King of Babylon, Nebuchanezzar. He gained understanding and depth of God's power and the ability to stand in awe of it, only after being severely humbled by God for seven years. I pray that God will continue to humble me so that I can stand in awe of Him, leaving no room for my own righteousness.

Chapter Seven - Instructions

And as I am humbled, it also helps be more mindful of my judgmental and righteous attitude. My poop scooping humility pie left a lasting impression that not only gave me the opportunity to increase my awe of God, but also increase my daily awareness of my sin. It creates in me a desire to make sure my words reflect Godly wisdom and not self-proclaimed knowledge. It resonates in me that I need to pray for Jesus to remove this sin. It speaks to my soul to humbly stand in awe of God everyday—no matter how full of poop I may think I am.

> With what shall I come before the Lord and bow down before the exalted God? Shall I come before him with burnt offerings, with calves a year old? Will the Lord be pleased with thousands of rams, with ten thousand rivers of oil? Shall I offer my firstborn for my transgression, the fruit of my body for the sin of my soul? He has showed you, O man, what is good. And what does the Lord require of you? To act justly and to love mercy and to walk humbly with your God.
>
> Micah 6:6-8

> Therefore, since we are receiving a kingdom that cannot be shaken, let us be thankful, and so worship God acceptably with reverence and awe, for our 'God is a consuming fire.'
>
> Hebrews 12:28-29

Obedience

One day as we were departing to my big kids' school, my little kids asked if they had to buckle their seatbelts. You see, we live very close to our school and I'm ashamed to say there are occasions where we don't always buckle up.

On this particular day, there was a police officer sitting right in front of us, so I told them they had to because of him. After we got home, I climbed onto my bike and the little kids climbed into the bike trailer and again they asked if they had to buckle, and I said no.

As I rode my bike along, a police car pulled out from one of the driveways and my little girl exclaimed that we had to stop so they could get buckled because there was a policeman.

It was in that moment I realized I was inadvertently teaching my children that they only have to obey the rules when an authority is there to enforce them. God used this wonderful enlightenment of what I was doing with my children and opened my eyes, as it applied to me, His child.

I seem to be very selectively obedient lately. I choose God's way sometimes and I choose the world's way other times—maybe more than God's way lately. But my husband made a statement that has really helped me begin to refocus my obedience. He said, "You can't pick and choose which commands of God you are going to follow."

And he's so right. I didn't say "yes" to Jesus on the condition that I could set my own rules. I said "yes" to Jesus and to all His commands and plans and expectations—to follow always, no matter who's looking.

The Bible is full of selectively obedient people and the consequences of their lack of obedience. And most of their choices were based on the same struggle I am fighting today—God's way versus the world's way.

I feel like the world's way is like quicksand, and once I make a worldly choice, I have a very hard time pulling my foot back out. I get consumed with the world and continue to choose the world instead of Jesus. The more I struggle, the more I get sucked in and lose sight of my loyalties. But if I can stop and become still, I can see Jesus, my lifeline, holding on to me. In that moment I am aware of His presence and my disobedience.

The choices I have made when I thought He "wasn't looking" or "wasn't there" are brought into the light and give me clarity on how good His way is and how wrong my choices are. Each time He pulls me out, it increases my obedience to Him—not because I know He's watching, but because I want to be for Him not the world.

"THEY WILL FIGHT AGAINST YOU, BUT WILL NOT OVERCOME YOU, FOR I AM WITH YOU AND WILL RESCUE YOU," DECLARES THE LORD.

JEREMIAH 1:19

Nakedness

If anyone would come after me, he must deny himself and take up his cross and follow me. For whoever wants to save his life will lose it but whoever loses his life for Me will find it.

Matthew 16:24, 25

Disguised

"My sins are weeds." This was my thought as I was out mowing and weeding my yard. I found myself amazed at and fascinated with the resiliency of the weeds I pulled up. Not only were they able to grow where grass or bushes weren't, but they were thriving in our drought conditions to the point of overtaking some of the grass and landscaping.

As I pulled weed after weed, I had to stop and look very carefully, as the weeds looked very much like the grass or bush they were trying to overcome. As I continued working, God confirmed my thought as He showed me how my sin carries the same qualities as these weeds.

Like the weeds that were hardly indistinguishable from the plants, my sin likes to disguise itself, trying to look like what Jesus wants me to be or do. My "busy-ness for Jesus" is . . . for Jesus. So what could be wrong with it? But just because something may look like it's for Jesus or from God doesn't always mean it is. Satan loves to use God's word in this way—twisting it just so.

He does this with Jesus in Matthew 4. Jesus is fasting for forty days when Satan comes to Him and uses a twisted version of God's word to try to make Jesus sin. Jesus rebukes Satan, but that doesn't stop Satan from using his manipulation and tricks on me. I have to know the difference between Jesus's truths and Satan's lies, and I can only do that by knowing God's word.

And when I'm not feeding my soul and heart, and heeding God's Word, there's an unfed hunger or empty space that can be filled by "other things"—worldly things. It is only a matter of time till these other things, like the weeds that grow where there's no grass, begin to crowd out the time and energy I should have for Jesus.

Jesus tells a parable in Luke 11:24-26 of a demon cast out of a person. This demon searches for a new home, but decides to return to the person he was cast out of. He finds the person "swept clean and put in order," but empty. So the demon invites his friends and fills the empty space. Jesus is letting me know that if I am not filling my empty space with Him, something else will fill it for me. God's word feeds the empty space in a way nothing else will be able to satisfy, not to mention it's great weed killer.

Finally, like those weeds, my sin is resilient—especially in spiritual drought. In the end, when the battle is over, I know who wins. Just read the book of Revelation. This book of the Bible gives us such hope as it describes what will happen when Jesus returns and the eternal living conditions that will ensue. *When Jesus returns–not if.* But until Jesus comes back with white robes flowing to fight the final battle, I have a daily battle to fight and cannot do it without arming myself with God's words every day.

In 1 Peter 5:8 it says, "Be self-controlled and alert. Your enemy the devil prowls around like a roaring lion looking for someone to devour." To be alert means be prepared to fight this battle—all the time. And what better way to fight it than with God's Word in my one hand and my shield of faith in the other. This is the best weed prevention there is.

Chapter Seven – Instructions

He humbled you, causing you to hunger and then feeding you with manna, which neither you nor your ancestors had known, to teach you that man does not live on bread alone, but on every word that comes from the mouth of the Lord.

Deuteronomy 8:3

Behold, I am coming soon! Blessed is he who keeps the words of prophesy in this book.

Revelation 22:7

EIGHT
For God

> Let us hold unswervingly to the hope we profess for He who promised is faithful.
>
> Hebrews 10:23

Jesus

My four-year-old twins brought home Jesus! Yes, you read correctly. Jesus. This Jesus doll was the "take home" thing for their preschool class. We were blessed to have Jesus in our home for a week where we could take pictures and write about our experience with Him before we returned Him to school. Let me tell you a little about how this visit with Jesus went …

On Thursday, upon His arrival, Jesus was the most sought-after thing in our house. He came with us everywhere, was the center of conversation, and was loved by all.

On Friday, He was still adored and toted around, but the excitement was ebbing.

By Saturday, Jesus was left on the floor, remembered occasionally, but mostly forgotten unless reminded of His presence.

By the next Wednesday, Jesus, unless He was seen, was completely forgotten. He was replaced by other toys and thoughts and only sought after at bedtime—if we noticed Him lying on the floor on the way there.

Nakedness

Notable thoughts about our visit with Jesus:

- This doll is not pretty, it's very ordinary and plain.

- As He was introduced to people, He became quite the conversation piece as people discovered He was a Jesus doll, but He was discussed as more of a joke than a bold proclamation of faith.

- The impact of Jesus at our house in a physical form probably had more impact on me than on my children.

Take a moment and reflect on my experience with the Jesus doll. How much looks like your relationship with Jesus? It unfortunately can look like mine sometimes.

I know Jesus is with me. Since He opened my eyes and my heart to what a relationship with Him looks like, His Spirit has lived in me. I needed a shabby-looking physical representation of Him, however, to make very clear that I don't live like He lives in me. The way my children loved Him and then forgot Him is such a great analogy to some of my days. In the morning, I'm charged up and ready to go and be bold and let Jesus shine through me everywhere I go, but throughout the day, I start doing my thing and trying to get it all done on my own, acting like He's not around—until I need Him or see my Bible.

Something that really stood out to me as I reflected on the visit from Jesus was how I would present the doll—here was an amazing opportunity to illustrate my faith to people, yet my explanation was one of a joke rather than the heartbeat in my life I claim Him to be. And this made me think about my kids and how they saw me introduce Jesus and laugh with the other adults. What was I teaching them?

I pray that after this experience with Jesus I can act as if I am carrying Jesus with me, every day, because I am.

Chapter Eight – For God

I HAVE BEEN CRUCIFIED WITH CHRIST AND I NO LONGER LIVE, BUT CHRIST LIVES IN ME. THE LIFE I LIVE IN THE BODY, I LIVE BY FAITH IN THE SON OF GOD, WHO LOVED ME AND GAVE HIMSELF FOR ME.

GALATIANS 2:20

AFTER THAT WHOLE GENERATION HAD BEEN GATHERED TO THEIR FATHERS, ANOTHER GENERATION GREW UP, WHO KNEW NEITHER THE LORD NOR WHAT HE HAD DONE FOR ISRAEL.

JUDGES 2:10

Trumpets

I love it when I'm doing my Bible study and I encounter one of those stop-in-your-tracks questions that makes me spend some quality time thinking and reflecting about what I am doing here. The Book of Revelation in the Bible is full of these opportunities.

In Chapter Eight there are about to be seven trumpets blown; as each trumpet is blown, it unleashes some form of destruction on the earth. God is using these disasters as a "wake up call" to those who still haven't pursued a relationship with Jesus. As I was studying these verses, my Community Bible Study question was, "What 'trumpets' has God used in your life to get your attention or call you to action?"

This question, in and of itself, was a trumpet call, because it really got me thinking about what God uses in my life to get my attention and call me back to Him. Here are a couple that come to my mind:

His Word—this is probably the one He continuously uses to grab hold of me. Every time I open my Bible, something convicts, something grabs me at the exact place I am and brings me back to Jesus. Hebrews 4:12 says, "For the word of God is living and

Chapter Eight – For God

active. Sharper than a double-edged sword, it penetrates even dividing soul and spirit, joints and marrow, it judges the thoughts and attitudes of the heart."

I go into His word a lost sheep and come out commanded and equipped to just follow Jesus. I go in burdened and frustrated and come out remembering to be joyful always, pray continuously, and give thanks for everything. His Word opens my eyes and my heart to what I have chosen not to see. It is always relevant and relatable to my life and never ceases to be a resounding trumpet that I need to pull me from the world and back to Jesus.

My Weaknesses—2 Corinthians 12:9 and 10 says, "But he said to me. 'My grace is sufficient for you, for my power is made perfect in weakness.' Therefore I will boast all the more gladly about my weaknesses, so that Christ's power may rest on me. That is why, for Christ's sake, I delight in weaknesses, in insults, in hardships, in persecutions, in difficulties. For when I am weak, then I am strong."

I struggle with boasting about my weaknesses, which is probably why they are the perfect trumpet for God to use to get my attention and get me back on board with His plan. When my weaknesses are brought to light, I am reminded I can't and am not supposed to do it alone. I am flawed and need Jesus in many ways, which helps keep me humble.

It also reminds me of the magnitude of God's love: "But God demonstrates His own love for us in this: While we were still sinners, Christ died for us." (Romans 5:8). He's going to use my weaknesses to remind me of all that He has done with my shortcomings and all that He will do through them, and it will be all for His glory, not mine.

Nakedness

Music—I am musical by nature, and God loves to use this to convict me and redirect me with a song. He always plays exactly what I need to hear on the radio in my car. He always sings the songs to make my heart cry out to Him at church. And He constantly gets a song stuck in my head that sings to my soul.

Exodus 15:2: "the LORD is my strength and my song; he has become my salvation. He is my God, and I will praise him, my father's God and I will exalt him." I love that He uses music to continually call attention to His faithfulness. Whether it be by answering prayer through lyrics or offering support through a chorus, He's telling me He's listening, and we will persevere together so keep my eyes on Him.

Friends—in For the City by Matt Carter and Darrin Patrick, it says, "that we come to know God more intimately in healthy, intimate relationships with other Christians who are seeking to know God. The multiple facets of who we are can only be uncovered in community, and despite what popular culture tells us, we were not meant to find ourselves on our own.

As individuals, we can't mine the depths of our greatest hopes, our worst fears, and the deepest desires of our hearts. Living in community and close relationship with other people reveals our strengths—that which makes us helpful to others—as well as our weaknesses—those things that makes us hurtful, our sinful patterns of behavior."

I had a friend apologizing, just the other day, because she felt she had overstepped her bounds and said too much. I assured her she had said exactly what I needed to hear and God had used her in a mighty way to give me clarity and direction. I find myself too often in her shoes though, or not in her shoes because I have held back something God had pressed me to say, because I thought it was too much. Who am I to filter God?

Chapter Eight – For God

God uses my friends and family to shine light on the dark places in my life and to keep me walking toward Him and offers me the same opportunity to be His light in their lives. These relationships are created "to spur one another on to good deeds" (Hebrews 10:24) and to create boldness for Him.

I pray that as you read this and reflect on your own life, God calls you to see how He is blowing trumpets at you, so that when you hear His call, you can run back to Him.

> I WAIT FOR THE LORD, MY SOUL WAITS, AND IN HIS WORD I PUT MY HOPE. MY SOUL WAITS FOR THE LORD MORE THAN WATCHMEN WAIT FOR THE MORNING, MORE THAN WATCHMEN WAIT FOR THE MORNING.
>
> PSALM 130:5,6

> FOR GOD SO LOVED THE WORLD THAT HE GAVE HIS ONE AND ONLY SON, THAT WHOEVER BELIEVES IN HIM SHALL NOT PERISH BUT HAVE ETERNAL LIFE. FOR GOD DID NOT SEND HIS SON INTO THE WORLD TO CONDEMN THE WORLD, BUT TO SAVE THE WORLD THROUGH HIM.
>
> JOHN 3:16, 17

Puzzles

I love puzzles! I have awesome memories as a child working on puzzles with my grandparents and parents and am now blessed with children who have a love of puzzles too. Just for clarification, I'm not talking about the kind of puzzles you find in the newspaper like crosswords or brain teasers. I'm talking about the kind that come in a box with a picture on it, and inside the box are about a thousand pieces of that picture that you have to connect and create.

I love starting a puzzle where all the pieces in their different colors, shapes, and sizes lay before me—there is no rhyme or reason as to how they lay on the table. Each piece is special in its own way, even though it might be nondescript until it is connected to another, which in turn begins to bring to life the small picture that is portrayed on the box.

Everyone who puts together a puzzle has the way they believe construction should go. I always start with the border—my grandfather insisted that you had to have that first. That way you knew where you could work within, it laid the foundation—the size and shape of what you are creating.

Next, you begin to find similar colors or pieces for a particular

Chapter Eight – For God

object. And as these sections come to completion, connections may be made between them, offering a glimpse of the picture that is being created. What remains are the challenging background pieces that all look the same. The task of finding where these pieces go can only be completed through tedious attempts of trying each piece in each spot.

When a completed puzzle lies before me, the sense of accomplishment and joy are always overwhelming. To take a bunch of little pieces and to construct a beautiful picture from the random is remarkable to me.

I feel my own life is like God's special puzzle. He takes random pieces that may mean something alone, but are most significant when put together and help me to see His greater purpose.

God has always been working on creating my border, but since I have come to call Jesus my Lord and Savior, I feel like He has laid the finishing "foundational" pieces that connect the border together—the pieces that show that I am new creation in Him. Those pieces that emphasize how it is all about Him and not about me. And even though my relationship with Him is fairly new and my border is in that fragile, unstable state of just being finished, He has already begun to place pieces together on the inside. Pieces that strengthen me and help me begin to see the picture He has planned for me.

He put Romans 8:28 on my heart: "And we know that in all things, God works for the good of those who love Him, who have been called according to His purpose." God works all things for the good of those who love Him. I've been internalizing that verse ever since I read it, trying to keep in mind that everything that happens, small, huge, horrible, or grand, is all working for my good.

Oswald Chambers connected a piece to that through his words

Nakedness

from *My Utmost For His Highest*: "The most important rule for us is to concentrate on keeping our lives open to God. Let everything else including work, clothes, and food be set aside. The busy-ness of things obscures our concentration on God. We must maintain a position of beholding Him, keeping our lives completely spiritual through and through. Let other things come and go as they will; let other people criticize as they will; but never allow anything to obscure the life that 'is hidden with Christ in God' (Colossians 3:3)."

I've been praying to behold God ever since I read this; to keep Him and His perspective of working everything for my good as the light in which I examine my situations. And I'm nowhere near perfect, but keeping God on my mind through all of life makes the difference as to whether I respond or react in a situation.

And the latest piece connected in my puzzle was from a sermon in church. My pastor asked us to pose the question to ourselves, "Why do we do the things we do?"

Previously, I'd asked myself a similar question, Paul's question: "Why do I do the things I hate?" While the latter question I have usually asked out of frustration and lack of success in staying away from sin, this new question is asked as a way to look at what I'm doing and glean insight into my motivation. I may have thought about using it when dealing with the "big stuff," but not about using it in my everyday.

Like: Why do I drive fast and cast judgment on other drivers because they drive in a different manner than I do? Is it for the glory of the Lord? Or is it because I pack my schedule too full and I am trying not to be late for everything?

Why do I get frustrated and raise my voice to my kids at 5pm? Is it because God has given me authority over them and I represent His Authority when I discipline them? Or is it because I'm tired and they're causing me great discomfort in their fighting and agitating each other?

Chapter Eight – For God

This question of why I'm doing things is proved invaluable, as everything I do should be to give God glory. If this is not occurring, then there is a disconnect somewhere, and I'm most likely not beholding and trusting in Him to work all things for my good.

God has laid His foundation—it's all about Jesus, not me. And now He has just begun to place His special pieces in my life, and as I see these pieces, connections are made that give witness to His faithfulness, trustworthiness, and love. (I don't know about you, but I can read about God's attributes all day long, and even though hearing them is insightful, my tangible experience with them is what really begins to bring clarity to the picture God is creating in me.)

God has a lot more pieces to put into place—some might not make sense, but He will link them and give me clarity and increased faithfulness through those connections in His timing.

In the meantime, I feel my trust in the Lord growing every day, as I know He knows the "picture on the box" and sees exactly what I'm going to look like when He's completed His workmanship in me.

> **FOR WE ARE HIS WORKMANSHIP, CREATED IN CHRIST JESUS FOR GOOD WORKS, WHICH GOD PREPARED BEFOREHAND SO THAT WE WOULD WALK IN THEM.**
>
> **EPHESIANS 2:10**

> **WE ALL, WITH UNVEILED FACE, BEHOLDING AS IN A MIRROR THE GLORY OF THE LORD, ARE BEING TRANSFORMED INTO THE SAME IMAGE…**
>
> **2 CORINTHIANS 3:18**

NINE
Likeness

Your attitude should be the same as that of Christ Jesus: Who, being in very nature God, did not consider equality with God something to be grasped; but made himself nothing, taking the very nature of a servant, being made in human likeness. And being found in appearance as a man, he humbled himself by becoming obedient to death—even death on a cross!

Philippians 2:5-8

Ordinary

I was reminded, one Sunday at church, that the Great Commission—"Therefore go and make disciples of all nations, baptizing them in the name of the Father and of the Son and of the Holy Spirit, and teaching them to obey everything I have commanded you. And surely I am with you always, to the very end of the age." (Matthew 28:19-20)—is not meant to be a burden, but to produce such a passion in me that I proclaim it to everyone, which will in turn complete my joy.

If I reflect on when I first found out I was pregnant… I was so excited to find out I was blessed with a child, but I got even more excited when I told people. In the sharing of my good news, my joy was complete! This is exactly the effect that telling people about the love I have for Jesus should have.

I should be so excited about the fact that Jesus died for me, taking on the punishment that was meant for me and my sin. That He then rose from the dead and now waits for me in heaven where I get to go and spend eternity with God.

These thoughts should fill me with such exhilaration that I can hardly contain this good news. But yet, I find myself not quite as joyful to proclaim my love for Jesus as I do for an expectant child, so I have to ask myself and implore God—why?

Why don't I always feel like proclaiming the Gospel in such a bold way? Why doesn't the thought of sharing the gift Jesus has given me regularly stir my passion? Why do I feel burdened by this command God has blessed me with to share the good news of the amazing salvation He has given me through His Son?

The answer, I think, is found in something I teach my Bible study students almost every week. Whenever I introduce a new person of the Bible to them, I try to emphasize how that person was an ordinary person, "just like you and me."

Mary was just a girl, nothing special about her. Matthew wasn't the nicest of guys. David was a sheepherder. Paul persecuted Christians, and Jesus still chose him. When I look at all the people God uses in the Bible, I see ordinary people that God made extraordinary.

When I look at myself, I see very ordinary, and find doubt instead of belief in the extraordinary. I fear instead of cleave. I cringe instead of being bold. I put God in a box confining Him to my human parameters, which makes the impossible, impossible, instead of the probable that all things are with Jesus.

I feel burdened instead of joyful because I feel unworthy and unequipped. So I stop at me and make my calling into a burden, instead of letting go of all my barriers and embracing God and the joy that is complete by proclaiming the good news to everyone.

But I am not asked to do this to make my life more difficult. God is with me and will provide all I need along the way. And He asks this of me to show the world His glory through someone who is ordinary, but becomes extraordinary through Him.

Chapter Nine - Likeness

Though you have not seen Him, you love Him; and even though you do not see Him now, you believe in Him and are filled with an inexpressible and glorious joy, for you are receiving the goal of your faith, the salvation of your souls.

1 Peter 1:8,9

For this is the love of God, that we keep His commandments. And His commandments are not burdensome. For whatever is born of God overcomes the world. And this is the victory that has overcome the world – our faith.

1 John 5:3,4

Grace

Holidays… tis' the season! And when the holidays begin, so does the baking. I love to cook and bake. God has truly gifted me here. I also love to teach, but as much as I want to pass down these loves to my children, I don't combine them well. In fact I'm incredibly challenged to show patience when I am teaching my children how to bake. But God gave me an opportunity to do both of these one Christmas while I was making apple pie.

Let me give you a little background on this particular apple pie recipe—it was passed down from my husband's grandma to his mom and then to me. In the Moore family, making apple pie is an art and a contest that is judged very strictly by those who indulge in the eating. There is always a score given to your pie. When I am making pie, it is not for the joy of the Lord, but for the highest score and approval of the family.

My oldest daughter told me she wanted to learn how to make apple pie, so this is where our story begins. She helped me cut apples, and she added ingredients, under my very strict instructions as to how to measure things and add things. All the while I scrutinized and watched her every move.

And then we came to the crust. Crust is very fickle—the less you mess with it the better it is. She was messing with my crust; I not so nicely asked her to stop, and at that moment she turned to me with big tears in her eyes and said, "I think I'm done." And she walked into her room.

Then I felt God nudge me to stop, (a lot nicer than I did to my daughter), and to ponder the question, is the result of my apple pie more important than my daughter's self-esteem? Deep Breath. I called her back into the kitchen, apologized, and explained to her that she was more important than the crust and I would love for her to continue helping me.

The grace I was unable to give my daughter is something I get regularly from the Lord—in such abundance, it is beyond what I can comprehend and far exceeding what I could hope to give.

It was in a recent study of Revelation 9:16-19 that my Community Bible Study opened my eyes to grace. As I read the verses, which describe a portion of God's destruction of sin, I reflected on the question that basically said this: If this is how God feels about sin, how do you feel about it?

My brain began a thought process, which immediately took me to Paul, in Romans 7:18-20: "I know that nothing good lives in me, that is, in my sinful nature. For I have the desire to do what is good, but I cannot carry it out. For what I do is not the good I want to do; no, the evil I do not want to do—this I keep on doing. Now if I do what I do not want to do, it is no longer I who do it, but it is sin living in me that does it."

I chased this rabbit trail down the slippery slope of self-defeat until I reached the "I think I am done" moment. In my convicted and saddened state at my inability to be as disgusted with my sin as God is, I discussed this with my husband who had a completely different perspective.

Nakedness

He saw Jesus's grace and love in the fact that, yes, we can't and won't ever be able to hate sin the way God does. And that is why we need God's grace. A grace we have because of Jesus. This should give me so much hope, but I can't always get past my self to see it.

When I am in my defeated, self-beaten–down mode, I am unable to do things for Jesus and I become useless to Him–exactly where Satan wants me. Too caught up in my self to remember God's grace. God takes these moments and shines His light into my life (like he did with my husband), calling me back to Him, saying, "It's ok—I know you have fallen short, but I have provided a way." Reminding me of His gift of grace.

With all the holiday hustle and bustle, I'm going to try to be not only thankful for, but also empowered by God's grace and use that empowerment to pass grace along to others, even if they are messing with my crust.

> **LOVE MUST BE SINCERE. HATE WHAT IS EVIL AND LOVE WHAT IS GOOD.**
>
> **ROMANS 12:9**

> **FOR IT IS BY GRACE YOU HAVE BEEN SAVED, THROUGH FAITH - AND THIS IS THE GIFT OF GOD - NOT BY WORKS, SO THAT NO ONE CAN BOAST.**
>
> **EPHESIANS 2:8C**

Preservation

A sweet friend of mine was sharing with me her father's story of growing up Jewish in France during the Holocaust. After all he endured and saw his family go through, this man found love and began to raise his own family. But because of the persecution he experienced growing up, he no longer lived out his Jewish faith; he lived a safer life, making sure not to draw attention to his heritage. His story grabbed a hold of my heart and had the question going through my mind: "This man preserved his life out of fear; why am I doing the same thing?"

I find myself living for this life more often then pursuing the life Jesus has offered me. The traditions and values I was taught have served me well as I am currently teaching them to my children—work hard, study for school, participate in activities—and you will grow to be a capable, functioning part of society.

Nothing too wrong with that. Some parts are Biblical, but the biggest part is missing. The Gospel, God's Holy Word, takes a backseat in the chaos—especially with my children. I make sure they have activities to do and that homework gets done, but time in the Word is infrequent. They may become functioning parts of society, but I want them to be functioning for Jesus and eternity, not for themselves and this world.

When Jesus told His disciples to "Follow me," they came immediately, leaving their boats, family, laundry, everything. I'm still working on scheduling my "following" in between swim lessons and gymnastics. I avoid following fully, by justifying my busyness with the be-in-the-world-not-of-the-world mantra. I claim that what I am doing is so I can "fit in," because I can't make an impact for Christ if I don't have an "in"–right?

Let's look at how Paul did it. He walked into a town, found a synagogue (his "in"), and preached there. Nothing happens so he heads to the streets where he has no "in," proclaiming the salvation of Jesus. People love it and commit their life to Christ.

This is a great reminder as I tend to perceive myself as having some sort of influence or control over who finds Jesus. The beauty of it is I don't. Look at all the pressure I just took off myself. I can go out and boldly proclaim the name of Christ and not worry about offending, because Jesus will do the rest. Jesus will lead me to the person He needs me to talk to and give me the "in" I need to make the connection.

Paul lived a crazy hard life that makes mine look like a walk in the park, yet he never faltered from proclaiming the name of Jesus. On the contrary, when I'm listening to praise music as I run or walk the trail here in town, I let the fear of someone I know see me, prevent me from raising my hands in the air in worship (which I always do in church, my car, or at my house, because I can't help myself).

Forget about the many who may see me and can relate and feel encouraged because they love the Lord too. Forget those who don't have a relationship with Jesus yet, and may be inspired to ask why I sing–giving me the opportunity to explain the reason for the joy in my heart. Forget that Jesus has loved and called and commanded me to boldly proclaim His name to help save the lost. Fear of ridicule holds me back, causing me to preserve the life I have created here.

Chapter Nine - Likeness

The verse I cling to and try to live by says; "I have been crucified with Christ and I no longer live, but Christ lives in me. The life I live in the body, I live by faith in the Son of God, who loved me and gave His life for me." (Galatians 2:20)

But I realize that I am not going to change overnight. Right now, I live for Christ when it fits my schedule and is convenient. "This life I live in the body, I live by faith", is sometimes, in the "Son of God", but most of the time it's faith in something created—me, family, things, etc. If I want to live by this verse it needs to be on my heart and mind constantly. Then hopefully, I will remember how much Jesus loved me enough to give His life for me. Why can't I give my life for Him?

I want to trust that Jesus can do things for Him better than I can. It's tough—I do things pretty well for Him now—not sure if He can do it any better. But maybe, I'll just surrender this life to Him and give Him a chance.

> Do not love the world or anything in the world. If anyone loves the world, love for the Father is not in them. For everything in the world—the lust of the flesh, the lust of the eyes, and the pride of life—comes not from the Father but from the world.
>
> 1 John 2:15,16

> Since you died with Christ to the basic principles of this world, why, as though you still belonged to it, do you submit to its rules.
>
> Colossians 2:20

TEN
The Unseen

For our light and momentary troubles are achieving for us an eternal glory that far outweighs them all. So we fix our eyes not on what is seen, but on what is unseen. For what is seen is temporary, but what is unseen is eternal.

2 Corinthians 4:17,18

Magic

This is a spoiler alert. I will be talking about Santa, and whatever you believe in Santa could be ruined if you read further.

My daughter has been asking sporadically over the last year if Santa was real, or whether I am Santa. And I have been diverting her questions by countering with the perfect mom response, "What do you think?" Which gave her the opportunity to think it out, out loud, and gave me the opportunity to let the subject be changed without lying outright to my child.

But alas, one night as she got ready for bed, this tactic was finally dismissed with her emphatic, "No I want you to tell me!" I delayed my daughter's bedtime and walked her out to my husband to have "the talk." I had her ask him the question, and after a brief stall of how proud of her he was that she came to us with her questions, he revealed to her that, no, Santa is not real and that her mommy and daddy were Santa.

The heartbreak that followed tore me in two. She began to cry, and I began to cry. She had believed so hard and had expected us to say that Santa was real—it was almost as if we blindsided her.

We talked about how the magic of Christmas hadn't changed, because Jesus is the reason for the magic. We discussed how she was now a part of the secret club that knew that mommies and daddies were Santa, and that she was sworn to secrecy to not share this information. But to no avail, her sobs continued as her heart broke for the destruction of this imaginary world that had been created for her.

She looked at us at one point and let us know that when she has kids, she is going to celebrate Hanukkah or something that celebrates just Jesus, because she didn't want her kids to have to go through what she was experiencing in that moment.

Dramatic, yes, but her point had been one I had been pondering myself. The mentioning of never creating Santa for her in the first place made me wonder whether I am leading my children astray by embracing this traditional, cultural fantasy.

Yes, we constantly bring home the point to my kids that Jesus is the reason for the celebration. But when they run out of their room Christmas morning, it is not full of anticipation and excitement to find Jesus underneath the Christmas tree. And even though the gifts under the tree are representations of the gift that Jesus is to us and the gifts that were given to Him, I don't think that is what they are thinking about as they rip through wrapping paper.

Last year, I was convicted about why we celebrate Christmas, with the climax for me being our amazing Christmas Eve service at church, and the anticlimax being Christmas morning—a huge change on my part since I have always loved Christmas morning. I was ready this year to pull the plug to let all the kids know that there is no Santa, the elf on the shelf does not really fly, and to make Christmas really about Jesus . . . and then my children started talking about and getting excited about the elf and Santa, which gained momentum.

So the elf came this year and all my kids were so into it (the other three still are). The excitement of my four-year-olds seeing Santa and racing to find the elf every morning was so fun. I too get lost in the magical world with my children and share the same struggle as my daughter of embracing Jesus as the magic of Christmas when we have been trained that toys and Santa is where the magic lies.

I have felt God using so many things around me to see Jesus as the true source of joy and magic of Christmas; to behold Christmas as a celebration of the birth of Christ and to begin to step away from traditions we have always known.

The shepherds knew and dropped everything to go worship Him. Mary knew and stored all the things that happened in her heart. The angels lit up the sky in multitudes with song and rejoicing. And why wouldn't they? Jesus Christ was born to save the world from sin. It is the beginning of the fulfillment of God's promise to save His children. How can a man in a red suit create magic greater than that?

> FATHERS, DO NOT EXASPERATE YOUR CHILDREN; INSTEAD BRING THEM UP IN THE TRAINING AND INSTRUCTION OF THE LORD.
>
> EPHESIANS 6:4

> LOVE THE LORD YOUR GOD WITH ALL YOUR HEART AND WITH ALL YOUR SOUL AND WITH ALL YOUR STRENGTH. THESE COMMANDMENTS THAT I GIVE YOU TODAY ARE TO BE UPON YOUR HEARTS. IMPRESS THEM ON YOUR CHILDREN. TALK ABOUT THEM WHEN YOU SIT AT HOME AND WHEN YOU WALK ALONG THE ROAD, WHEN YOU LIE DOWN AND WHEN YOU GET UP. TIE THEM AS SYMBOLS ON YOUR HANDS AND BIND THEM ON YOUR FOREHEADS. WRITE THEM ON THE DOOR FRAMES OF YOUR HOUSES AND ON YOUR GATES.
>
> DEUTERONOMY 6:5-9

Blessings

~~~~~~~~~~~~~~~~~

God wasted no time one New Year to show me how He can bless me in the most unlikely ways.

The entire family climbed into the car for our five-minute ride to church, and by the time we got there, my husband looked at me, a little green, and said, "I don't feel all that great." So we drove him back home and I returned to church to hear a wonderful sermon which highlighted Romans 8:28: "And we know that God causes all things to work together for good to those who love God, to those who are called according to His purpose."

I really wanted to digest and take to heart this verse—look at all this verse is saying: whether things are good or bad, God is in control, and even though I may not see it today or ever, He is using all the things in my life for my good to help me grow in my relationship with Him and live for His glory. That's a lot packed in to one verse, and a lot to let go of and trust the Lord with.

When we returned from church, my husband was lying on the couch going through chills and fever and had a very upset stomach; by 5pm he was vomiting. By 12am my oldest daughter followed suit. She and I were up all night as she got rid of

Chapter Ten - The Unseen

everything in her system, and then continued to dry heave for another three hours.

The entire night, instead of being consumed with exhaustion, frustration, and fear, I had God's perfect peace. It was truly amazing. I focused on the Roman's verse, trusting God was in control and He was using this for my good. I knew He was going to get me through. And He did. The next day my husband felt like new, my daughter was recovering, and it looked like we were about done with the stomach bug and God had showed such great faithfulness. I felt on fire with passion and trust for Him!

Now this horrible little virus had entered our house a week before with my two youngest children getting sick, but theirs was a one-time-get-it-out-of-my-system-and-I'm-done bug. So they had had it. Now two more of our family had had it; that left two of us who hadn't fallen to the sickness yet, and I was pretty sure my middle son wouldn't—he just doesn't do stomach bugs (lucky him). I was fighting it like a champ. At 3 o'clock the next day, I knew I had lost.

I had walked my two girls to the library and was standing there helping them find books when it literally washed over me. I had to go home—now. We quickly walked home and as soon as I walked into my house I curled up in bed where I stayed, for the most part, till the next day.

I laid there, in and out of sleep, hot and cold, queasy and sick, praying. Not a prayer of desperation, but a peaceful prayer. A prayer of praise and thankfulness. Prayers for my friends and family. Prayers for my life. Every now and then I would pause in my prayers and listen.

I listened to my husband take care of my kids. And let me tell you what I heard: I heard a man figuring out what each child wanted for dinner and then sweet conversations as he prepared it for them. I heard my older son pray to bless the food. I heard happy voices and content hearts.

This sweet time was not only peaceful, but very revolutionary. God pointed out to me that my family doesn't need me, and I

Nakedness

don't mean this in a sad way. I mean it in a liberating letting-go-of-having-to-control-everything way.

In the past when I have been sick, I have also been covered with guilt and frustration and worry about who was going to do what I was supposed to be doing. And in this moment, God let me see that life does function just fine without me controlling it. He has it all under control, and I can trust Him with the people I find precious, since He finds them precious too.

I know in the past I would have looked at this situation and thought about how it was a sign that the year was going to be a bad one, but I perceived this as gift from God. He used this sickness for my good. He helped me see how when I trust Him, I have His peace, no matter the circumstances. He also reminded me of how trustworthy and sovereign He is. What a blessing—something I never thought I would say about the stomach flu.

> DO NOT BE ANXIOUS ABOUT ANYTHING, BUT IN EVERYTHING, BY PRAYER AND PETITION, WITH THANKSGIVING, PRESENT YOUR REQUESTS TO GOD. AND THE PEACE OF GOD, THAT TRANSCENDS ALL UNDERSTANDING, WILL GUARD YOUR HEARTS AND YOUR MINDS IN CHRIST JESUS.
>
> PHILIPPIANS 4:6,7

> AND WE KNOW THAT GOD CAUSES ALL THINGS TO WORK TOGETHER FOR GOOD TO THOSE WHO LOVE GOD, TO THOSE WHO ARE CALLED ACCORDING TO HIS PURPOSE.
>
> ROMANS 8:28

A Moment

I'd like to share with you what my husband and I did one New Year's Eve—it's a confession of sorts.

We began our evening at a nice little vegan restaurant for dinner, which was followed by one of our favorite date night activities—sitting on the patio of Whole Foods with a nice bottle of wine and a good loaf of fresh bread. (Yes this causes me much pain and discomfort since neither of those things agree with my body, but I always justify it with the thought that it is just one night.)

After the wine and bread had been consumed, we then engaged in, what I am ashamed to say, is one of our other favorite date-night activities: walking up and down the main party drag in town to pass judgment on those who have "dressed up" or "liquored up" and are now walking around in the street.

We only share our comments between us; we don't ridicule people to their faces, only behind their backs, so that's ok right? No, it's not, and we know it is wrong, and are convicted, but are unable to stop once we start. This night, there were even Christians in the middle of the street with a bullhorn, handing out flyers to help people find Jesus. As we passed them, and I turned down their flyer, I said, "I love Jesus!" … but I sure wasn't acting like it.

I tell this story of momentary self-exaltation at others' expense not only to confess my sins, but also to show how God truly convicted me of the damage that this occasional "fun" can cause through my study of Revelation.

As I read Revelation 13, it tells of the "beast" Satan summons out of the sea. My Bible study takes me to several places in Scripture to reveal other names and descriptions of the beast. In 2 John:7 he is referred to as the Antichrist, "the man doomed for destruction" and "the man of lawlessness" from 2 Thessalonians 2:3, and "the abomination that causes desolation" in Matthew 24:15.

These descriptions of this man are written in the Bible for all to see, including the man who is going to play this role. The way I understood this is that the Antichrist, even with the knowledge of his destiny (doomed to destruction), still wages everything for momentary worship and exaltation. He does become worshipped as God is and is given the power and authority over the nations, but only for a short time.

He will then spend eternity in the lake of fire. He has full knowledge of what will happen, yet partakes anyway because what is offered now is fun and better than where he was a moment ago. Momentary glory for eternal damnation.

This thought of momentary glory is a driving force in our society today—risk it all for that one glorious moment. So many people seem to be looking for that one moment that will bring them fame and glory for a blink, knowing or unknowing of the consequences that that moment will cost them.

I am guilty of this. One of those moments of seeking glory or feeling superior over people is in the fun and giggles of a night judging others—seems harmless, but isn't it in these small things that God asks us to be faithful, that God calls us to rise above the "harmless" sinful acts, so when the temptation of the greater sinful acts crouch at the door, we are prepared to not give in to the temptation?

Chapter Ten - The Unseen

I know it sounds silly, and I know judging others one night with my husband will not land me in the lake of fire, but could it? No sin is "harmless". God despises all sin. And I don't want to ever think otherwise because just writing this has made my heart ache at my own sin.

Seeking my one glorious moment is not one I want to find on earth. The moment I want glorified is as I stand before God and rest in the knowledge that I glorified Him and not me. I trusted in all that He has done for me, and all He has prepared for me is far more glorious than anything I could ever attain here on earth.

As a side note, since I wrote this, my husband and I were both incredibly convicted and have changed our favorite date night activity to something both healthier for my body and our souls.

> IF WE DELIBERATELY KEEP ON SINNING AFTER WE HAVE RECEIVED THE TRUTH, NO SACRIFICE FOR SINS IS LEFT, BUT ONLY A FEARFUL EXPECTATION OF JUDGMENT AND OF RAGING FIRE THAT WILL CONSUME THE ENEMIES OF GOD.
>
> HEBREWS 10:26, 27

> DO NOT JUDGE AND YOU WILL NOT BE JUDGED. DO NOT CONDEMN, AND YOU WILL NOT BE CONDEMNED. FORGIVE, AND YOU WILL BE FORGIVEN. GIVE AND IT WILL BE GIVEN TO YOU. A GOOD MEASURE, PRESSED DOWN, SHAKEN TOGETHER AND RUNNING OVER, WILL BE POURED OUT INTO YOUR LAP. FOR WITH THE MEASURE YOU USE, IT WILL BE MEASURED TO YOU.
>
> LUKE 6:37,38

ELEVEN
Fasting

> Set your mind on things above, not on earthly things. For you died and your life is now hidden with Christ in God.
>
> Colossians 3:2-3

Control

All I wanted was a parking place! But alas, for the past fifteen minutes I had been driving around to no avail. I was getting frustrated. My big kids were in the beginnings of a wrestling match in the backseat. My little kids were verbally letting me know they wanted out of their seats now. So I did exactly what any reasonable mother would do—I lost it, turned around, and gave my children a rather loud request for them to settle down and help look for a parking place.

I was so frustrated because I had no control—no control over the availability of the parking places and no control over the kids, which lead to no control over my own actions.

There it was, my idol of control. This is my heart's deep desire to have everything under my watchful eye and proceed exactly as I have planned, instead of letting go and letting God be in control.

My awareness of the particular idols I have in my life had been heightened as it was the season of Lent. This particular Lent, I had felt that in order to prepare my heart for Easter, I would fast on only five foods for the forty days. As I started this adventure of limiting what I was eating, my thoughts behind it were to grow a deeper relationship with the Lord by removing my food/comfort idols. And yes, the Lord is drawing me nearer to Him, but He's really digging out all the juicy, yucky stuff that needs to go, like my secret desire to have control.

I was surprised to see this control thing. In my everyday life I am a pretty laid back, go-with-the-flow, "punt"-type person. I never even thought I had made it an idol; I was wrong.

I have found that even though I may be okay with punting, it is in the controlled chaos type of way—I have controlled the parameters of the chaos. When the chaos is just plain chaos, I am very uncomfortable, and my frustrations tend to run very high. Here is where I get lost in the feeling that nothing is going as I have planned and usually end up spiraling down with that.

Now I know I have this ugly idol, so the next step is a confession of sorts: "Hi, my name is Sandra, and I am not in control." The step after that would be to give it to God, who has always had it anyway. He knows all that has happened, all that will happen, and all that is happening. Total control. So why do I fight Him for it? Why can't I trust Him?

I can answer both those questions with one word—pride. There it is again! Crazy ugly pride. My pride tells me that if I'm not controlling things, it won't get done right. Or if someone else is in control, they most certainly need my expertise to get it done. My husband loves this one (yes, that is sarcasm).

But all my pride really does is continuously get me in the way of God. I need to humble my head so I can get it through my heart that God's got it, not me. Hopefully, then, I can trust Him to run with it; He's going to do it the way He has planned, and He's working it all for my good, so I might as well let go.

Amidst all this, I have gained a new understanding of being "still." I've written about how God wants me to still my body and mind for Him, to hear Him and grow my relationship with Him. What hadn't occurred to me before is that when my mind is actually completely still I am not trying to control anything. I have given everything to Him in that moment. It is in those moments of absolute stillness that I am showing God I trust Him to be in control.

Whether I am organizing an activity, wrangling my kids, or trying to find a parking spot, I am not in control. God is. And He truly can work it all out so much better than I can.

> THOSE WHO LIVE ACCORDING TO THE SINFUL NATURE HAVE THEIR MINDS SET ON WHAT THAT NATURE DESIRES; BUT THOSE WHO LIVE IN ACCORDANCE WITH THE SPIRIT HAVE THEIR MINDS SET ON WHAT THE SPIRIT DESIRES. THE MIND OF SINFUL MAN IS DEATH, BUT THE MIND CONTROLLED BY THE SPIRIT IS LIFE AND PEACE; THE SINFUL MIND IS HOSTILE TO GOD. IT DOES NOT SUBMIT TO GOD'S LAW, NOR CAN IT DO SO. THOSE CONTROLLED BY THE SINFUL NATURE CANNOT PLEASE GOD.
>
> ROMANS 8:5-8

> WHAT, THEN, SHALL WE SAY IN RESPONSE TO THIS? IF GOD IS FOR US, WHO CAN BE AGAINST US? HE WHO DID NOT SPARE HIS OWN SON, BUT GAVE HIM UP FOR US ALL – HOW WILL HE NOT ALSO, ALONG WITH HIM, GRACIOUSLY GIVE US ALL THINGS?
>
> ROMANS 8:31, 32

God's Feast

I love camping! One Spring break we were blessed to go camping with two other families—six adults, thirteen kids, and two dogs.

We went to the best campsite ever. No cell phone service, no running water on site, and compostable toilets a quarter mile away. We filled our time with float trips down the Colorado river, hikes to waterfalls and natural springs, fishing, climbing trees, hanging by the campfire, and all the joy and fun living in community brings. It was an amazing experience. God was there throughout it, but before I even left, He was preparing me for the work He was going to do in me.

As we were driving to the campground, I was reflecting on Daniel—particularly about when Daniel chose not to eat the king's food. This is a passage I have read more than I can count, and studied three times, but only through the insight I gain from the experiences God puts me through can I truly glean what these verses offer.

In Daniel 1:3-6, 8-16, Daniel and his friends have been taken to Babylon and chosen to be trained for serving the king's court, which included a daily ration of the king's choice food and three years of education. Daniel and his friends decided not to eat the food, but request vegetables and water. In the end they end up performing better than the other boys. This summary is so you know the story, but picture this:

A table full of the king's food, the best of the best—smells that wafted into the air from the prepared meats, the bounty of breads and sides and wines that would be offered, succulent desserts of every kind—and Daniel looks at the bountiful buffet and says, "I would prefer water and vegetables."

Then he sits alongside these other young men and eats his vegetables and drinks his water for ten days. His reason was not to offend the Lord, and because of this dedication to God, he looked and performed better than those indulging in the feast. Let me tell you how this was vital to me during this camping trip.

We had awesome camping feasts. We may have been roughing it, but we all love good food and it was in abundance. But at every meal, because of the commitment I made during Lent to only eat five foods, I cut up my apple and sprinkled some almonds on it or put my beans and rice in a pot and added some spinach.

This is not a woe-is-me statement. It was done with the same perseverance that Daniel went about eating his vegetables and water. Not once did I have a pity party about only eating five foods, but only focused on the commitment I had made to the Lord, to grow closer, to gain insight . And He rewarded me with a new understanding of Daniel, a glimpse of how much of what he had done was not easy, but accomplishable with the right motivation and the right help.

His motivation was to not defile his body, honoring his relationship with the Lord by not indulging in foods that were deemed "bad." My motivation was to gain a closer relationship with the Lord, and by doing so to eradicate my horrible relationship I have with food.

As I departed for this trip, I had to pack enough beans, rice, spinach, apples, and almonds for three days. I rationed it out daily, being deliberate about when I ate and the portions and snacks, and you know what, I didn't feel like I was missing anything. I wasn't craving, wasn't hungry. I was busy and knew I only had so much. I adjusted to what I actually needed versus what I was trying to fill time and void with.

But as soon as I walked through the door of my kitchen when we got home, I made a beeline for my almonds like a starving woman. Even though almonds were something I could eat, the feeling of desperation overtook the peace so I overindulged at the first opportunity I had. In that moment God just let the situation sink in—the irrational thoughts I have in regards to food, how I fill time with it, how I have habits that even with my limitations I'm still indulging in, how I still use food instead of Him. I had to be taken away from it all to not only see, but also to understand how I let food define my existence and hinder my relationship with Jesus.

Daniel had the right kind of help. It says, "God granted Daniel favor." God was there with Daniel, helping to strengthen Daniel and give him the opportunity to be faithful. Through this, God has reminded me that I cannot make these changes in my habits, only He can.

When I am eating normally, I have a lot of self-determination and "rules" I set for myself in regards to food. The rules I set are always broken because they are rules I am trying to do on my own. I haven't been faithfully praying for God to take this, to help me look at food as a source of nourishment instead of the never-ending feast, and I think that's the best place to start.

Dear sweet Jesus,

Thank you Lord for giving me Daniel's story to look to, and for the abundance of food you have provided for my enjoyment. I'm sorry I struggle with making food into a substitute for You. You were kind enough to put me in the woods where I had no choice, but to rely on you for my strength and perseverance. And then You brought me to my regular world and showed me how, when I have food at my disposal, I have no control. I pray, God, that You will turn my thoughts and heart to You, and my desperate need for food will dissipate into a desperate need for You.

Chapter Eleven – Fasting

> Since you died with Christ to the basic principles of this world, why, as though you still belonged to it, do you submit to its rules: 'Do not handle! Do not taste! Do not touch!'? These are all destined to perish with use, because they are based on human commands and teachings. Such regulations indeed have an appearance of wisdom, with their self-imposed worship, their false humility and their harsh treatment of the body, but they lack any value in restraining sensual indulgence.
>
> Colossians 2:20-23

> So do not fear, for I am with you; do not be dismayed, for I am your God. I will strengthen you and help you; I will uphold you with my righteous right hand.
>
> Isaiah 41:10

Cravings

As Easter approached, I began to get bombarded with the question, "What are you going to eat?" A thought that really hadn't crossed my mind as eating only five foods had become a way of life. So as I began to really think about this question and digest the fact that I was going to re-enter the world of consuming more than five foods, I became fearful.

Fearful of going back to being a habitual eater. Fearful of choosing the right foods for my body. Fearful of losing my new perspective on food. And to be honest, fearful of gaining back the weight I had lost.

Saturday night, the night before Easter, I was washing the dish I had used to make rice for the last forty days. The dish slipped from my hands in the sink, broke, and cut my hand. I felt like this was God's way of letting me know there was nothing to fear, He was in control and as long as I focused on Him and His plans for me, He would take care of the rest.

I have learned so much over the time I limited what I ate—I had many "aha!" moments, but none as profound as when the dish broke, because, even though I hadn't told anybody, He knew my fears. He knew I was fluctuating between just eating five things forever and creating a whole bunch of rules for food. And He knew my limitations and rules were not what I "needed."

I've been trying to put rules on my eating for a long time. I've done this to help the way I feel and to maintain my weight. I can't eat this or that or past a certain time or alone—all these rules are the cause of the problematic relationship I have with food.

The answer to all this, as with everything, is in the Gospel. Jesus never meant for us to live following a bunch of rules. That was what the Pharisees had created—a lifestyle of dos and don'ts that determined whether or not you could go to heaven. We are not bound by dos and don'ts. There are no rules to living for Jesus. He loves us, while still in our sin. He died for us, and now He has risen and is alive, wanting us to love and obey because we are loved. He wants my heart to be so full of Him that I don't desire to live any other way than the way He has called me to. Not with rules to follow, but out of love and adoration of Him who has given me life.

Just as Jesus doesn't want rules for my way to worship Him or live for Him, He doesn't want me to define the things I do in my life by rules I have created for it. He wants me to be all consumed with Him. To be so full with Him that my desire is for Him and not food, that food takes its rightful place in my life as . . . food.

So I re-enter the world of food consumption slowly, holding tight to Jesus as I ease back into the "waters of choice." And the most awesome part is that He is holding me just as tightly.

> ALL OF US ALSO LIVED AMONG THEM AT ONE TIME, GRATIFYING THE CRAVINGS OF OUR SINFUL NATURE AND FOLLOWING ITS DESIRES AND THOUGHT. LIKE THE REST, WE WERE BY NATURE OBJECTS OF WRATH. BUT BECAUSE OF HIS GREAT LOVE FOR US, GOD, WHO IS RICH IN MERCY, MADE US ALIVE WITH CHRIST EVEN WHEN WE WERE DEAD IN TRANSGRESSIONS – IT IS BY GRACE YOU HAVE BEEN SAVED. AND GOD RAISED US UP WITH CHRIST AND SEATED US WITH HIM IN THE HEAVENLY REALMS IN CHRIST JESUS, IN ORDER

THAT IN THE COMING AGES HE MIGHT SHOW THE INCOMPARABLE RICHES OF HIS GRACE, EXPRESSED IN HIS KINDNESS TO US IN CHRIST JESUS. FOR IT IS BY GRACE YOU HAVE BEEN SAVED, THROUGH FAITH – AND THIS NOT FROM YOURSELVES, IT IS THE GIFT OF GOD – NOT BY WORKS, SO THAT NO ONE CAN BOAST.

EPHESIANS 2:3-9

A MAN REAPS WHAT HE SOWS. THE ONE WHO SOWS TO PLEASE HIS SINFUL NATURE, FROM THAT NATURE WILL REAP DESTRUCTION; THE ONE WHO SOWS TO PLEASE THE SPIRIT, FROM THE SPIRIT WILL REAP ETERNAL LIFE. LET US NOT BECOME WEARY IN DOING GOOD, FOR ALL THE PROPER TIME WE WILL REAP A HARVEST IF WE DO NOT GIVE UP. THEREFORE AS WE HAVE THE OPPORTUNITY, LET US DO GOOD TO ALL PEOPLE.

GALATIANS 6:7B -10A

TWELVE
Hard Pill

> Only let us live up to what we have already attained.
>
> Philippians 3:16

Teachable

I was at the grocery store on a Sunday. Now I don't usually frequent grocery stores on Sundays, but we had no food, so I joined the rest of the world at this particular grocery store with a very tight time frame to get in and get out. For those of you who already avoid the grocery store on Sundays, I would advise you to continue to do so, because it's a zoo.

I made it through the store in record time and headed to the checkout lanes, which is where I met the reason I don't shop on Sundays—crazy lines! I surveyed the scene, made, what I thought was a very wise decision, and got into a line.

There were three people ahead of me in line. One was paying, one of them had all their stuff loaded on the belt, and the cute young couple in front of me only had half a basketful, so I'm thinking, "No worries." Totally could make it through the line fast and be on my way. I kept telling myself the Lord had control, I was not going to stress about where I had to be or how much time I had to get there. Then the couple in front of me begins to unload their cart. They unload half of it and then put up a little divider to show separate orders—that's not good.

Then they unload two-thirds of what is left and put up another divider—even worse. Now the belt is full and they have to wait before they can finish unloading their basket. I feel my pep talk about who's in control begin to dissipate, so now I'm praying—God is in control, nothing I can do, no need to stress.

When they finally finish unloading their third batch, they line everything up in two rows on the belt, so their two rows of ten items take up the whole belt. They inform the checkout guy that they have found expired items and have brought the expired items and the matching non-expired items, which they would like to get for free, and laid them out just so.

This is where I lost it. My kids (I had three of the four), seeing my now blatantly obvious frustration, which I was no longer trying to hide, asked why, and I said out loud, "Mommy chose the wrong line. These people are taking forever!"

As soon as those words were out of my mouth, I regretted them. This cute little couple had heard me for sure, and they moved as fast as they could to get out of there. By the time I looked up from unloading my cart they were long gone and I was left with the feeling of shame.

And that awful feeling wouldn't go away. I confessed the whole scenario to my husband and it helped, I begged for forgiveness from God and that made it better, but then I just sat with God and let Him speak to me through things I read and heard.

He used the words of Oswald Chambers in *My Utmost for His Highest* (March 16): "Live constantly reminding yourself of the judgment seat of Christ, and walk in the knowledge of the holiness He has given you. Tolerating a wrong attitude toward another person causes you to follow the spirit of the devil, no matter how saintly you are."

Judgment is something I have written about before because I struggle with it, a lot. But God used these circumstances and Chambers's words to really speak to my heart on what is occurring when I judge others. I have the wrong attitude, and that attitude is one that follows Satan.

Chapter Twelve – Hard Pill

God reminded me of how He made us all different, and it is those differences that make us all unique and wonderful. But yet, it's one of those differences I chose to pass judgment on, rather than learn from and embrace. Jesus is the only Judge, and I pray He can help me to reserve the judgment of others for Him.

God then used a sermon from my church where the pastor talked about "Lordship" in our lives. He spoke about how Jesus is our Lord, and if that is truly true, then He should have complete control, leadership, authority, and power over my life. Complete is the key word.

In my scenario, I felt like God was in control as long as things were working in my favor, but when they went south, I decided I should probably take control, as if to say, "I gave you a chance and you didn't come through, so now I'll do it my way." God reminded me that I don't just do this in line at the grocery store, I do it every day of my life and it's time for me to stop thinking I can take it from Him.

Lastly, God gave me *The Screwtape Letters* by C.S. Lewis. This book is brilliantly written from Satan's perspective and offers some insight into Lewis's thoughts on human nature. At the end of the first letter, which is from Satan (Screwtape) to his nephew Wormwood, a demon, he says this: "Thanks to the process which we set at work in them centuries ago, they find it all but impossible to believe in the unfamiliar while the familiar is before their eyes. Keep pressing home on him the ordinariness of things."

I catch my eyes settling on the familiar and ordinariness way too much. And sometimes the schedule, the hurriedness, all things that have to be done, becomes so much my ordinary that I can miss the unfamiliar–walk right past the God factor that is constantly working in every facet of my life . . . like how God was actually teaching me, in the grocery store, how to be more frugal.

Nakedness

If I'd gotten my panties out of a bunch, I could have asked this sweet couple about what they were doing and how they went about getting thirty-plus dollars worth of free food. Which, even more amazingly, could have turned into an opportunity to speak the Gospel into their lives.

God uses the unfamiliar to teach me, to grow me, to give me wisdom and insight, and to give me opportunity so that even though, compared to the world, He may seem unfamiliar and unseen, the more I let Him teach me, the more familiar and seen He becomes to me.

But God didn't leave me there trying to fix myself or berate myself for being a sinner. He brought me back to what I have to do—repent and pray. There's nothing I can will myself to do, there's no way for me to change me, but I can choose to get quiet and let God be the Lord of my life, to ask Him to strengthen me against my wrong attitude, for me to persevere against the familiar and the ordinary, and to trust Him with all that is unfamiliar and unseen.

> BUT I TELL YOU THAT MEN WILL HAVE TO GIVE AN ACCOUNT ON THE DAY OF JUDGMENT FOR EVERY CARELESS WORD THEY HAVE SPOKEN. FOR BY YOUR WORDS YOU WILL BE ACQUITTED, AND BY YOUR WORDS YOU WILL BE CONDEMNED.
>
> MATTHEW 12:36-37

> YOU, THEREFORE, HAVE NO EXCUSE, YOU WHO PASS JUDGMENT ON SOMEONE ELSE, FOR AT WHATEVER POINT YOU JUDGE THE OTHER, YOU ARE CONDEMNING YOURSELF, BECAUSE YOU WHO PASS JUDGMENT DO THE SAME THINGS.
>
> ROMANS 2:1

Extra

Sunday morning I had some great quiet time with Jesus. I read Scripture and then I got on my knees and prayed. I can't remember the last time I got on my knees to pray. There is something powerful about being in such a humbled position. And with the prayer I prayed, I could feel the Spirit working it through me.

I prayed for help with my food struggle, particularly that I wouldn't eat "extra." "Extra" for me is that extra couple of bites I take of whatever I'm eating—the bites that don't go into the dish. For example, when I make myself a cup of coconut yogurt and almonds, I put a couple handfuls of almonds in the yogurt and another couple handfuls of almonds in my mouth . . . "extra."

I prayed I would trust in what God had provided me and not go for the "extras." I also prayed, from the depth of my soul, for God to change my heart—that it would beat for Him and His glory alone. Powerful prayer time! It was 8:30am, and I was ready for the day.

The next hour and forty-five minutes became brutal. I had left my kitchen a disaster from the night before, so I began with getting my yogurt and almonds and tackling my kitchen. As I put the almonds in my yogurt and then put them away, I didn't get any extra.

I was trying to clean my kitchen when my four children and husband wanted breakfast, which means my kitchen becomes a restaurant—a bowl of oatmeal, a bacon sandwich, toast with cinnamon, Chex cereal, a breakfast taco. While I'm trying to clean my kitchen and make food for everyone, my children start coming with new requests—"I need socks!" "I have no underwear!" "Do you know where my shoes are?" "Can you braid my hair?"

At one point I was trying to do something for five other people at once—six if you include the fact that I was trying to clean my kitchen for me. On top of all this, I was also trying to watch the clock so we could get to church on time. Praise God! God kept me strong against getting "extra," but as we arrived at church late, I was wishing I had had extra almonds and a little less of all the requests, because I was drained.

So I walked into church fighting tears. I had let a couple sobs out in the shower, but I was really working hard to not let the feelings of being completely wiped and depleted from the hairiness of the morning overcome me. I was saddened that my precious time with Jesus from only a short time earlier seemed to have been wiped away.

But if I'm being honest, I was mostly disappointed. Here I had spent some awesome time with Jesus, and I felt as though I hadn't been rewarded for it—the quality time felt as though it should have had some result attached to it, but yet my morning was tough and I didn't feel any different spiritually.

In this state, I stood in church, unable to sing, and if I can't sing I pray. God didn't have me stand there long before His answer came. He said, "Isn't this what you asked for?" And in that moment He blessed me by opening my eyes and allowed me to understand what He had been doing—He had been working on my heart. He had been answering my prayer.

God gave me an opportunity that morning to change my heart by looking for me to give everything I was doing to Him. By allowing

Chapter Twelve - Hard Pill

me to struggle, but empowering me to not go for "extra," God is showing me His faithfulness, provision, and trustworthiness, and strengthening my heart to be for Him.

And by Him meeting me here, at church, God is making sure I comprehend that His way of answering my prayers may not be what my idea of answer to prayer looks like. I still think that a lightning bolt moment or having a holy hill meeting will change me overnight, but He's reminding me that He uses my everyday as His Holy Hill to transform me and give me the opportunity and the strength to focus on Him and not my circumstances. To lean on Him and not myself.

I cried at that point. I had my eyes shut so tight and the tears just poured out the sides. I was so overwhelmed—not with the things of this world, but in that moment I was overwhelmed by God's love for me. I was overwhelmed with all the "extra" He had given me in answer to my prayers, and how He is always working on my heart. To Him be all the glory!

> IN THE SAME WAY, THE SPIRIT HELPS US IN OUR WEAKNESS. WE DO NOT KNOW WHAT WE OUGHT TO PRAY FOR, BUT THE SPIRIT HIMSELF INTERCEDES FOR US WITH GROANS THAT WORDS CANNOT EXPRESS. AND HE WHO SEARCHES OUR HEARTS KNOWS THE MIND OF THE SPIRIT, BECAUSE THE SPIRIT INTERCEDES FOR THE SAINTS IN ACCORDANCE WITH GOD'S WILL.
>
> ROMANS 8:26,27

Nakedness

While I was speaking and praying, confessing my sin and the sin of my people Israel, and presenting my plea before the LORD my God for the holy hill of my God, while I was speaking in prayer, the man Gabriel, whom I had seen in the vision at the first, came to me in swift flight at the time of the evening sacrifice. He made me understand, speaking with me and saying, "O Daniel, I have now come out to give you insight and understanding. At the beginning of your pleas for mercy a word went out, and I have come to tell it to you, for you are greatly loved. Therefore consider the word and understand the vision.

Daniel 9:20-23

THIRTEEN
Leap

Be joyful always; pray continually; give thanks in all circumstances, for this is God's will for you in Christ Jesus.

1 Thessalonians 5:16-18

Mine

My husband and I went on a wonderful trip for our 15th wedding anniversary. It was full of many adventures, and while there was no physical "need" for God, He was there in such a tangible way, continuing to pursue me, bringing to light some amazing things.

The first day on our trip, we went to a town that had the largest Banyan tree in the world—it covered almost an entire acre. This tree, like most, has one trunk but as it grows, the roots come down out of the individual branches to support them. The tree ends up looking like it has many trunks.

Under this tree sat a man who appeared homeless. He overheard my husband and I talking about the history of the tree and town as we walked past him, so he started talking to us about the facts he knew. It was then I noticed he had a Bible on his lap, which is eventually where our conversation turned.

His knowledge of Scripture was inspiring. He would read from the Old and the New Testament, working through the intricacies of the Bible the way you know the back roads of your town. It was incredible. And the stories of his life he told were also quite remarkable.

Nakedness

One story remained on the forefront of my mind though. It was about his friend, Philip, who would wait until everyone else had been fed to go and get his food from the food trucks that came to feed the homeless. Simple story, great message.

The following day we had signed up for a special tour where we were "promised" the best seats. But, alas, we ended up in what many travelers had described as "the worst seats." So for the first ten minutes I pouted. I struggled to keep my bitterness and frustration at bay. Finally I lifted it all up to Jesus, because really there were no bad seats and I was doing something new and exciting. I got over myself and enjoyed.

The third day, God started to link everything together. As we were on our way to our next excursion, I pulled out my copy of The Valley of Vision, which is a book of Puritan Prayers. I'd never opened this book, and I flipped randomly to a prayer called "happiness," and this is what it said:

> Help me to never expect happiness from the world, but only in thee. Let me not think that I shall be more happy by living to myself, for I can only be happy if employed for thee, and if I desire to live in this world only to do and suffer what thou doubt allot me. Teach me that if I don't live a life that satisfies thee, I shall not live a life that will satisfy myself.... Help me to not think of living to thee in my own strength, but always to look to and rely on thee for assistance. Teach me that there is no greater truth than this, I can do nothing of myself.

Huge light bulb moment! God in that moment connected the dots. From the story of Philip to the tour ride to this moment to my daily life, I'm always making sure to take care of me to make sure I get what I deserve to ensure "happiness." That hurts to write. But it's true.

I make sure that I have the food I need, the best seats, the routes planned... my world functioning in the way I know works well.

Chapter Thirteen - Leap

Rarely do I trust God enough to leave room for Him to provide, to work things out for my good. I make sure it is "good" to begin with.

God expanded on this as I sat and read Matthew with my husband. Jesus says in Matthew 16:24-25: "If anyone would come after me, he must deny himself and take up his cross and follow me. For whoever wants to save his life will lose it, but whoever loses his life will find it."

Deny myself—whether it is food or the best seat, I always have me as my motivation in my mind. And isn't that the irony of the whole thing? I still live my life as if it is mine, when in actuality nothing is mine—I deserve nothing, but only because of Jesus' denying of Himself do I get what He deserved. Brings tears to my eyes—the mighty sacrifice He made for me, and how little I offer to Him in return.

> DO NOTHING OUT OF SELFISH AMBITION OR VAIN CONCEIT, BUT IN HUMILITY CONSIDER OTHERS BETTER THAN YOURSELVES. EACH OF YOU SHOULD LOOK NOT ONLY AT YOUR OWN INTERESTS, BUT ALSO THE INTERESTS OF OTHERS.
>
> PHILIPPIANS 2:3-4

> IF ANYONE WANTS TO BE FIRST, HE MUST BE THE VERY LAST, AND THE SERVANT OF ALL.
>
> MARK 9:35

Eye Contact

Have you ever seen a movie or show where one of the characters is trying to get another character to cross a particularly treacherous path? The scenario usually plays out where the braver character ends up making eye contact with the one afraid and either uses humor or romance or some form of distraction to get the other across.

Like the scene in Shrek where there is a rope bridge and Shrek backs donkey across it, keeping eye contact with him and teasing him. Or the third chipmunk movie (forgive me, kid's movies are all I know) where Simon helps Janette cross a log bridge by gazing deep into her eyes and flattering her as they cross. These are on my mind as I reflect over the many fears I faced on my recent trip and how Jesus helped me overcome those fears by directing my gaze to Him.

Even though most of my fears from our trip were physical, like jumping off thirty-foot sea cliffs into a pool of spring fed water below, or going on eco-adventures that could result in crashes and death, they were all things God used to show me I should have no fears when I keep my eyes on Him.

He brought me to the place where I could take a moment, look

Chapter Thirteen - Leap

up, and pray, "OK Jesus, we're doing this together," before I would take the plunge into the next adventure. With my eyes on Him I was washed over with the knowledge that He was with me, and whatever happened, He had control over it. It also gave me an amazing peace and an added exhilaration to the adventure.

With my eyes on Him, He got me across my bridge of fear on my vacation, but also reminded me this is where I should focus daily. When my fears may stop me in my tracks from the things Jesus has called me to, I often don't recognize that I'm letting my fear of the unknown overcome my trust in Jesus, which turns my gaze away from Him.

Another thing—on these adventures my husband and I adopted a "When are we ever going to do this again?" philosophy. And as I reflect on that now, I'm thinking it's the same philosophy I should be living my life for. I only have this one life to live, and too often I look my fears in the eye and say, "No way" rather than look to Jesus and say OK!

I know He's where my sights should be set—all the time, looking straight at Him—not worried I will stumble, because I will, and He'll pick me up. Not worried I will fail, because I will, and He will use it to help me grow and succeed in Him. Not worried about who's watching or what I have here, because He is preparing a place for me, and He is the only one who matters. Jesus has blessed me with this life to live for Him; there is nothing that I should fear.

On my trip there was a place that reflected all this perfectly. My husband pointed it out—it is his analogy and I'm just going to expand upon it. This particular place we found off the beaten path. We climbed down a two-hundred-foot rocky terrain hill to get to sea level where there were tide pools.

Now tide pools in and of them selves may not sound very exciting, but these tide pools were formed by holes in the hardened lava rock, so there was a jagged wall of lava where the twenty- to thirty-foot waves crashed over and fed these tide pools. The biggest pool was probably about ten feet deep and the size of two small Jacuzzis.

Nakedness

As we swam in this completely tranquil and calm pool, the waves were literally crashing over the rocks all around us. While we were in and near the pool there was no danger, but a few steps too close to where the waves would crash over the lava wall and you would be swept out to sea or crushed against the rocks.

In the pool is where we are supposed to live our lives. The pool was an amazing reflection of the perfect peace and calm of Jesus that I have when I am trusting in Him and looking at Him, even when the world around me is turbulent, ferocious, and a little scary, and can sweep me into it if I get too close. But as long as I stay close to Jesus, focused on Him, there is nothing to fear, there is no death, but only the life He is giving me to live here and eternally with Him.

> **PRAY ALSO FOR ME, THAT WHEN EVER I OPEN MY MOUTH, WORDS MAY BE GIVEN ME SO THAT I WILL FEARLESSLY MAKE KNOWN THE MYSTERY OF THE GOSPEL, FOR WHICH I AM AN AMBASSADOR IN CHAINS. PRAY THAT I MAY DECLARE IT FEARLESSLY AS I SHOULD.**
>
> **EPHESIANS 6:19-20**

> **WHAT IS IMPOSSIBLE WITH MEN IS POSSIBLE WITH GOD.**
>
> **LUKE 18:27**

Discomfort

My oldest daughter was trying out for a big musical production in our town. Her first audition she was full of her confident, true-to-herself self, which is what probably landed her the second audition. But I was surprised to see her become nervous and self-doubting as we walked up to the building for the second tryout.

As I was struggling to find the words to boost her confidence again, God stepped in and He decided to speak through the story of David and Goliath.

David, the youngest of eight boys, just a kid, heard Goliath mock God, and that was all he needed to have the courage to fight Goliath. He wasn't the biggest guy or the strongest, didn't have the best armor or come from a connected family, he was just David the little brother of some soldier (yes, the anointed king too, but David didn't rely on that part).

He took five stones, a slingshot, and his faith in God out to the battlefield. There were probably no shouts of encouragement, but a lot of snickering and doubt that this kid was going to do any good. David let nothing deter him though. He boldly went out, completely unafraid, not to show off for anyone, not to prove he was the best, but to exemplify God's sovereignty and glory.

This is what I shared with my daughter. And of course, as the Spirit spoke to her through me, it spoke to me too. Why do I struggle with that kind of trust? That kind of boldness? Why can't I wake up every day, put on God's armor, and say, "You come against me with sword and spear and javelin, but I come against you in the name of the Lord Almighty...!" (1 Samuel 17:45).

The world may not have a physical sword or spear, but the obstacles I face sometimes feel as sharp and deadly as one. And I certainly don't always take them on in the name of the Lord. No, I try to fight my battles on my turf and terms, and God showed me, through David's life, one of the reasons why.

A friend said something very wise and Godly-timed to me: "God doesn't move me unless I am content where I'm at." Not comfortable, but content. If you look Biblically at David, he was content—anointed king as a kid, and he returned to the fields not in a complaining sort of way, a God's-timing sort of way.

When he served Saul, the current king, even though David had been anointed king to succeed Saul, he did so humbly and devotedly, seemingly content in God's plan and sovereignty. And then as Saul pursued David, continuously trying to kill him, again David had mind-blowing trust and peace about God's direction for his life, not trying to take matters in his own hands, even when given opportunities to do so.

None of these situations had David in his comfort zone, yet he found contentment among the opposition and turmoil—in God and His Sovereignty.

Discontentment entered David's life when he didn't trust God's sovereignty and tried to rectify his earthly unhappiness on his own (2 Samuel 11). David had made it through so many tough times trusting in God, but he let his physical discomfort get the best of him.

I, unfortunately, pursue my own contentment daily—whether it is food or my children or my schedule, I am seeking comfort, not

Chapter Thirteen - Leap

the Lord's will for my life. I'm not always looking for God and His purpose in my frustrations and irritations as much as I'm trying to find my happy place again.

But God is working through these trials, through the discomfort. God is letting me know through David's example that as I become more content through the uncomfortable times, it strengthens my relationship with Him and enables me to stand in the daily battles, without doubt, without question, and say, "I come in the name of the Lord."

> I AM NOT SAYING THIS BECAUSE I AM IN NEED, FOR I HAVE LEARNED TO BE CONTENT WHATEVER THE CIRCUMSTANCES. I KNOW WHAT IT IS TO BE IN NEED, AND I KNOW WHAT IT IS TO HAVE PLENTY. I HAVE LEARNED THE SECRET OF BEING CONTENT IN ANY AND EVERY SITUATION, WHETHER WELL FED OR HUNGRY, WHETHER LIVING IN PLENTY OR IN WANT. I CAN DO ALL THIS THROUGH HIM WHO GIVES ME STRENGTH.
>
> PHILIPPIANS 4:11-13

> BUT THOSE WHO HOPE IN THE LORD WILL RENEW THEIR STRENGTH. THEY WILL SOAR ON WINGS LIKE EAGLES; THEY WILL RUN AND NOT GROW WEARY, THEY WILL WALK AND NOT BE FAINT.
>
> ISAIAH 40:31

FOURTEEN
Justified

And whatever you do, whether in word or deed, do it all in the name of the Lord Jesus, giving thanks to God the Father through Him.

Colossians 3:17

Excuses

My son loves to play video games. He is passionate about it—too passionate, as he gets incredibly emotionally attached to the game he is playing. Because of this emotional investment, he tends to make excuses for when he isn't playing well. "I didn't push that button," "I meant to jump," "The turtle made me do it," and so on. I've never seen a child so admittedly deny something that he caused as much as when my son plays video games. It is never his fault, and if he owns up to it being his fault, he never goes down alone.

Thinking about his stream of excuses made me think about the things I "excuse" in my own life—justifying my way around where I should be Biblically and where I want to be like the world. But, as I pondered how I "justify" things, there came a realization that there is a big difference in the definition of the words "justification" and "excuse," and neither are to be used with God.

"Justification" is defined as the act of showing something to have reason, an explanation, a rationale. "Excuse," on the other hand, is an attempt to lessen the blame attached to a fault, seek to defend. (Google dictionary). I found that the word "justify" can be a synonym of "excuse," but not the other way around. I will clarify with a Biblical example:

Nakedness

In 1 Samuel 15, Samuel tells Saul, the one God has chosen as the first king of the Israelites, to go and attack the Amalekites and "totally destroy everything that belongs to them. Do not spare them: put to death men and women, children and infants, cattle and sheep, camels and donkeys." (v.3). Saul sets out and does as the Lord commands, except spares their king and the best of the sheep and cattle. So the Lord lets Samuel know He's not happy because Saul "has not carried out my instructions," (v. 11).

Samuel heads out to talk to Saul about all the Lord has told him, and on his way to finding him, discovers Saul has set up a monument in his own honor. Samuel finally catches up to Saul, and Saul is excited about how he has followed the Lord's instructions. He's obviously pretty proud of himself in this moment.

But Samuel calls him out in a mighty way. Samuel reminds him what the Lord has done for him and that he didn't obey what the Lord had called him to do. Saul's reaction was an attempt to justify, but really he's just making up excuses. He says in verse 20: "I did obey the Lord, I went on the mission the Lord assigned me. I completely destroyed the Amalekites and brought back their king (not part of the instructions). The soldiers (placing blame somewhere else), took sheep and cattle from the plunder, the best of what was devoted to God, (not all), in order to sacrifice them to the Lord God at Gilgal (sucking up)."

He does not have "rational reasons" behind his excuse—he has a lot of relocating the blame and defending what he did. And that's what Samuel says to him. "Does the Lord delight in burnt offerings and sacrifices as much as in obeying the voice of the Lord? To obey is better than the fat of rams. (you messed up, own up to it! and repent!). (v22)."

Then, as Saul grovels for forgiveness, Samuel simply lets him know there's no forgiveness here: "You have rejected the word of the Lord, and the Lord has rejected you as king." (v.26).

Deep breath!

I love this passage for all that is in there to learn from, and I don't like this passage for the conviction it brings. I feel like

Chapter Fourteen - Justified

God is calling me out through it. He is letting me know my "justifications" have no "reasons" that hold any ground. I'm truly just giving excuses, redirecting blame for my disobedience.

The crazy thing is that God has already redirected the blame "once for all," (1 Peter 3:18). He sent Jesus. He placed all my sin—past, present, and future—on Jesus, who was sinless, and then killed Him and my sin. Internalize that for a moment. And now Jesus, who rose from the grave, stands at God's right hand advocating for me. Yet, I still can find an excuse to sin.

But isn't that the perfect justification? It's true and a great explanation! I can say "I'm a sinner," just like my son's "excuse" is, "It's not my fault." God's grace has me covered. I'm ok to sin. NO. There are so many things wrong with that thought. Defending my sin is saying it's not bad–it is bad because all sin is against God! Also, when I excuse away my faults, I'm taking away the opportunity from God to use my weakness to show His strength.

And lastly, excuses are not repentance. I'm not seeking the Lord's favor; I'm looking to make myself look good, which makes me look bad. I'm covered in sin, trying to excuse it away, but now I'm just covered in excuses and sin, not washed white with snow as when I repent.

Like my son, the more passionately and emotionally tied to my sin I am, the more excuses I have, and the less often God gets the glory He deserves. I want to be more passionate for God than for my sin, so really, there is no excuse.

> **For Christ died for sins once for all, the righteous for the unrighteous, to bring you to God. He was put to death in the body but made alive by the Spirit.**
>
> **1 Peter 3:18**

> **Direct my footsteps according to your Word; let no sin rule over me.**
>
> **Psalm 119:133**

In Crowd

My oldest daughter planned her birthday party guest list based on the people she had most recently interacted with, which meant she invited "new friends" (girls who she had only played with once), over friends she has had for years. I, being her protective mother who suffers from the need for approval, tried to convince her to add her "old friends" out of my fear of social backlash, but she wanted to invite who she wanted to invite.

So I stepped back and let her do her thing, until there were some "no" replies. Then she came to me with requests to invite these other friends that I thought she should have in the first place. And I'm ashamed to say I actually thought about and started to compose e-mails to do so, but the voice of reason from my husband brought me back to the reality that inviting these individuals as the backups would be worse than not inviting them at all.

The party ended up being a huge success. The hodge podge of people she invited were exactly who was supposed to be there. Which just proves God works more easily through my daughter than me. She does not get caught up in the "social etiquette," but invites those God has put in her life, in that moment. It's in this

Chapter Fourteen - Justified

innocence and lack of concern for approval from the world, that she lets Jesus' love shine through her.

My heart does not have this sweet innocence, and God used her to remind me that He has put me here, where I live, for a reason—His reason. I am called to make an impact for Him, not try to fulfill my "need" of being accepted by the dark fallen world.

I read Romans 12:2: "Do not conform any longer to the pattern of this world, but be transformed by the renewing of your mind. Then you will be able to test and approve what God's will is—his good, pleasing, and perfect will." Which reminded me that conformity is much easier than transformation, especially when you are transforming into something that is against the social norm.

A Biblical man whose life was against the social norm was David. David's life celebrated God, followed God, centered on God. He was a man of prayer. He went straight to God on almost every decision, and it wasn't a negotiation, it was a question looking for an answer—God's answer.

And God's response dictated his path. He embraced every decision God made as his own.

Too often, I go to God to have Him bless a decision I have already made. My decisions are based on what I see as best and are usually motivated by the culture I live in and the socially acceptable response to things. Then I pray, "God, please bless this and make it happen so my life may continue on in this wonderful manner and people will like me!" A little different than David.

Through His Word, God is asking me to come, humbly, to Him for His plan –to inquire the direction for my life. He then commands me to go and present His plan to those around me. It's in this moment of trust and obedience that I will find His perfect peace in every social situation that will allow me to answer the question, "Who are you trying to please?" with an unwavering, resounding, "You, Lord."

Nakedness

When I came to you brothers, I did not come with eloquence or superior wisdom as I proclaimed to you the testimony of God. For I resolved to know nothing while I was with you except Jesus Christ and him crucified. I came to you in weakness and fear and with much trembling. My message and my preaching were not with wise and persuasive words, but with a demonstration of the Spirit's power, so that your faith might not rest on men's wisdom, but on God's power.

1 Corinthians 2:1-5

Dear friends, do not imitate what is evil but what is good. Anyone who does what is good is from God. Anyone who does what is evil has not seen God.

3 John 11

Elevating

I love teaching fourth-grade girls about the Bible. The profound things they say always amaze me and challenge me to have "faith like a child." In light of having "childlike faith," God has begun using the lessons I am preparing for them as a way to bring me to a deeper place of understanding of who I am and who He is.

As I taught the girls about sin, I found a wonderful visual example to help them understand what sin is. First, we defined sin as "anytime you put yourself in the place of God." Then we began to create our visual aid.

I had one child stand on a chair as a representation of God, and another child stood on the floor, symbolizing humanity. I then gave examples of what sin would look like in their lives (eye rolling or disrespecting parents, not following rules, or not doing things they were supposed to).

After the "sins" were named, I asked the girl who was "humanity" to step onto a chair, putting her in the same place as God, symbolizing what we do when we sin.

There they stood, the one girl as God and the other as humanity on equal ground. A visual representation of how we elevate ourselves to Godly heights even though we are just His creation. I hope this visualization has stuck with the girls as much as it has stuck with me.

In my life, God took this example and has expanded upon it to really increase my understanding of how bad my sin is. He has opened my eyes with Philippians 2:5-8: "Your attitude should be the same as that of Christ Jesus: Who being in very nature God, did not consider equality with God something to be grasped, but made himself nothing, taking the very nature of a servant, being made in human likeness. And being found in appearance as a man, he humbled himself and became obedient to death- even death on a cross!"

After reading these verses, the depravity of my sin, the magnitude of what I am doing when I sin, began to sink in. Look at verse 6: "Who being in very nature God, did not consider equality with God something to be grasped."

Jesus was God, but was so humbled He didn't consider Himself even worthy to think about being God. Ponder that for a second and then think about the last time you "put yourself in the place of God." I elevate myself to God's place daily, and not in a holy, faithful way but in an I'm-going-to-be-God-now way. I've never thought of my sin as "that bad" before.

And God knows I don't think sin is all bad, so He continued to point out in the next verses to explain what my attitude should be. Verse 7 and 8 describe how Jesus not only humbles Himself, but because He found Himself in human likeness, he became a servant and obedient to death.

This is the example Christ set for me—not flippancy toward sin, but humility and obedience to God to the point I die to my sinful ways. Unfortuanately, I'm not very good at humility or obedience. I have a prideful streak in me that views humility as weakness. And I fight daily to die to myself, or choose God's desires for me over my selfish desires. These statements I just made show exactly what God is trying to get me to see—to see how deep my sin is.

Chapter Fourteen - Justified

Since I only seem to grasp these concepts on a moment-by-moment basis, God decided it was time to rearrange my moment by moment. Our family was temporarily down to one car—four kids, a husband who drives out of town for work, and my schedule with one car.

Besides a lot more biking and walking for the kids and me, this also brought a new perspective—a what's-really-important perspective, a slow-down-and-spend-time-to-disciple-my-children and a more-time-with-God perspective. There were things we missed, activities that were not participated in, more time spent to drop off and pick up, and a lot more time at home.

Humbly, I submitted to this plan that God had put me in, and I have to say it was precious. The time spent was cherished and unhurried, and I like to think I took a leap toward the Lord and maybe even died a little to myself. But guess what? I got my car back soon after, and with the car, my perspective shifted back, and I put myself right back up on that chair next to God.

Frustration and disappointment screamed from my soul, but God is kind enough to let me know that this is exactly where He wants me to be. Because until I hate my sin the way He hates it, it will always look and taste and smell better than what He is offering. What to do?

Continue to repent and continue to seek Him. I also need to tell you about my attempts to be on that chair. This is not only humbling, but it brings my sin into the light, elevating God onto the chair and me, humbly at His feet.

> FOR WHOEVER WANTS TO SAVE HIS LIFE MUST LOSE IT, BUT WHOEVER LOSES HIS LIFE FOR ME AND FOR THE GOSPEL WILL SAVE IT.
>
> MARK 8:35

Nakedness

When you were slaves to sin, you were free from the control of righteousness. What benefit did you reap at that time from the things you are now ashamed of? Those things resulted in death. But now that you have been set free from sin and become slaves to God, the benefit you reap is holiness, and the result is eternal life. For the wages of sin is death, but the gift of God is eternal life in Christ Jesus our Lord.

Romans 6:20-23

FIFTEEN
Shoulders

Come to me all who are weary and burdened, and I will give you rest. Take my yoke upon you and learn from me, for I am gentle and humble in heart, and you will find rest for your souls. For my yoke is easy and my burden is light.

Matthew 11:28-30

Disciples

I went to an informational meeting about a University model, Classical Christian School that is starting in my area. This type of school teaches kids to be thinkers, educating kids using techniques that help to gain knowledge rather than just retain information for a test. It also carries the common thread of the Lord throughout all the subjects.

If you're learning about Moses, you're learning the history of the people in the region and the geography of where he lived and reading books that are related to that too. I love this way of teaching, and the thing that really made me fall in love with the whole concept is it helps me to be faithful to God in His call for me to "raise up disciples." They used this term in the meeting, and it was a great reminder that our children are our disciples.

Hearing that phrase again made me reflect on how I am doing in equipping my children to be disciples. And if I'm being honest with myself, I am falling way short in this area.

Our church does an incredible job of equipping us and providing us materials to work with our kids during the week. I take these materials home and think about how I'm going to incorporate them into our daily lives. But the week starts and the materials get put into "the pile," where I find them on Saturday as I'm cleaning.

Then there are times I'll get ambitious and write out Bible verses for my kids to memorize. These valuable pieces of paper end up in the recycle bin within a day or two, covered in sticky substances.

There are devotionals for kids, Bibles for kids, and Bible studies for kids, and I always have a good intention of reading, and teaching, but I usually get too caught up in all the other stuff we do to bring it to fruition or make it part of the routine.

As I'm praying about what to do with my children's education and discipleship for the coming years, I am also praying about how God wants me to disciple them now. God has made me realize that it doesn't matter if they get Jesus in their education if they aren't getting it reinforced at home.

When Jesus is the center of our life at home, it increases the chance that He will be the center of our life as we go out. Just like when Jesus sent the disciples out to tell the nations, they would gather to Jesus, hear His teachings, have their lives centered on Him, and then go away from Jesus and share the Gospel—share Jesus with the world. Then returning to Him, they would get refreshed, renewed, and then off again.

We don't have Jesus waiting for us at home in the same way the disciples did, but we have His Word to spend time in, to learn from, and to refresh ourselves with, and His Spirit to call on to teach, strengthen, and empower us—powerful tools to equip us to be His disciples.

I can teach my children to read the Word and call on the Spirit, but really, the best way they learn is by watching me. Paul writes continuously about how his greatest testimony is the way he lives out his life to everyone he meets in his travels.

So my children's knowledge of what discipleship looks like comes from my behavior—scary. Do they see how I go to food instead of the Lord for comfort, control, and approval? Do they see a parent who is slow to anger and extends the grace and forgiveness of Jesus? Do I show a love for Jesus as the sole reason for everything

Chapter Fifteen - Shoulders

I do? The answer to all these questions is "sometimes," which means I need to be in the Word and centering my life on Jesus every day.

God has called me to raise up disciples—to bear fruit, ten, thirty, one hundred fold. He has given me the privilege of this task—another task He does not need my help for, but one He has graciously asked me to do. For if I'm raising disciples for Him, I am being the disciple He has called me to be.

> Fix these words of mine in your hearts and minds; tie them as symbols on your hands and bind them on your foreheads. Teach them to your children talking about them when you sit at home and when you walk along the road, when you lie down and when you get up. Write them on the door frames of your houses and on your gates.
>
> Deuteronomy 11:18-20

> So whatever you eat or drink or whatever you do, do it all for the glory of God. Do not cause anyone to stumble, whether Jews, Greeks, or the church of God - even as I try to please everybody in every way. For I am not seeking my own good but the good of many, so that they may be saved. Follow my example, as I follow the example of Christ.
>
> 1 Corinthians 10:31 - 11:1

Hit

I ran out the door to pick up my little kids after sending an e-mail about a fourth-grade girls' Bible study I'm starting. Between that and plans in the afternoon to go and help with a new Bible study for elementary kids in a city near mine, I really felt the need to pray out loud in my car as I drove.

I was almost to my kids' school, and had just finished praying, "Submit yourselves, then, to God. Resist the devil, and he will flee from you." (James 4:7), when I realized what I had done.

The traffic light I had just gone through was red, and out of the corner of my eye, I saw the car coming. For a split second, I thought I was going to make it—I was wrong! He slammed into the back driver side tire and spun me 180 degrees, turning my car the wrong way on a one-way street and deploying my side air bags.

I don't remember a lot, but I do remember letting go of the steering wheel and closing my eyes. I let go of trying to control anything in the situation and gave it all to God. And God came through in a mighty way!

Praise God I was the only one in my car, and both the man who

Chapter Fifteen - Shoulders

hit me and I walked away without injury.

Praise God I was only hit by the one car, and that there were no other vehicles traveling on the road around me, so I hit no one else when I spun.

Praise God I was in my husband's vehicle and not my car (which is the only car that holds the whole family), and my husband was available to come help me and pick me and the kids up.

Praise God for the people He put in place to offer the grace and encouragement He knew I would need.

God showed me how this was Satan's defensive tactic to my offensive prayer—to shake me, to get to me emotionally. Satan knows that I can easily be coerced into dwelling on the fact that this was my fault, that I had caused this man and my family a lot of disappointment, and that I was an absolute failure.

Satan has this talk with me a lot, and he had it ramped up ready to go. But God was there with the perfect pep talk! He used all the people around me to speak truth into my life. The guy I hit gave me a hug! The police officer and the director of the preschool both told me how they had recently run red lights; the man at the front desk of the preschool told me how there was an accident on that corner once a week. And my husband . . . he was so compassionate and sweet about the whole thing.

What Satan tried to use for bad, God used for good. This is essentially what Joseph says to his brothers in Genesis. Joseph's brothers sold him into slavery, which leads to a lot of horrible circumstances and a rough life for Joseph.

But God, through the experience, changed Joseph so when the day came for his brothers to stand before him begging for forgiveness, he was able to say, "You intended to harm me, but God intended it for good to accomplish what is now being done, the saving of many lives." (Genesis 50:20).

And God did the same for me. He created so much good in what Satan was trying to use to cause me harm. First, I was able to look at the situation and see how God was in absolute control—there are so many things that could have gone horribly worse, and they didn't.

Second, the accident served as a reminder that my identity and value comes from God, not from anything in this world, and especially not from my husband. I felt bad for all that had happened at the scene of the accident, but I felt even worse about having to tell my husband what I had done. Even though he continually responds to my goof ups with grace and love, I still am overcome with feelings of shame and guilt because I feel like I have caused him grief and let him down.

Lastly, I gained perspective on life. As I sat at home that night and reflected on the, "What if I had died...," my first thought was about how dirty my house was. So I immediately got up and cleaned the toilets. But then I really thought about the impact I make daily.

What were the last impressions I would have left on friends and family? Had I completed what God had sent me to do, or had I wasted too much time and fallen way short? Have I produced Spiritual fruit?

As I pondered these questions, I found some good answers and some not-so-good answers, but ultimately I heard the Spirit re-emphasize the intentionality I should be living with. Today is what God has given me to shine His glory and make disciples for Him. There is no time to waste, but only a sense of urgency to live fully for Him every second of every day.

I pray that the things God taught me through this experience I can hold on to as I go through my daily life. I want to focus on His Sovereignty, my identity in Him, and the intentionality to live boldly for Him. The experience has been a blessing, and the fact I get to share it with you is the icing on the cake.

Chapter Fifteen - Shoulders

Be on your guard; stand firm in the faith; be men of courage; be strong. Do everything in love.

1 Corinthians 16:13-14

But seek first his kingdom and his righteousness, and all these things will be given to you as well. Therefore do not worry about tomorrow, for tomorrow will worry about itself. Each day has enough trouble of its own.

Matthew 6:33-34

Proficiency

When my husband travels out of our city by car, he takes my stylin' minivan and leaves me his '78 Ford F250 pickup truck. (This is the arrangement we've had since I totaled his car, not because he loves driving my minivan.)

It's a great truck, but it is big, old, and has very loose steering, which makes it very intimidating for me to drive. Imagine if you will, hands at ten and two on the steering wheel and then constantly moving the wheel back and forth to stay straight in this very wide and large vehicle, on very narrow roads.

The awesome part of this situation is it causes every fiber of my being to have complete dependence on Jesus while I drive. "Drive your truck, Jesus, drive your truck," is the only thought in my mind as I weeble-wobble down the street. Driving the truck is something I don't think I'll ever master or become complacent in relying on Jesus to do, but I was recently reminded that when I perceive something that I do for Jesus as "mastered," I may be more wobbly at it than I think.

I had been fasting on a weekly basis for a couple months, so when my husband asked me to fast on a particular day with him, I of course said yes. I had been fasting regularly because I find if I'm

Chapter Fifteen - Shoulders

fasting, I'm much better at surrendering to God. I don't say this to you to boast of my righteousness and holiness, I say it because I need you to understand that I have become very proficient in fasting–and that is a self-righteous statement, which is exactly where the problem began.

As I began fasting with my husband, everything was off to a good start. I thought about God and prayed about all the things He was doing through my husband. It didn't take long though to revert to a suffering/excuses fast. By noon I was dying! At four o'clock I went to green tea to help me persevere, and at 5:15 I threw in the towel, thanked God, and ate lots of handfuls of pepitas to break the fast.

To emphasize how much my mind, heart, and soul were not where they were supposed to be, let me tell you what happened after the pepitas. I ate two bowls of salad, a fish taco on a flour tortilla (I'm a gluten-free vegan so that makes no sense), another bowl of salad, and a cup of applesauce with cinnamon and almonds—almost a whole days worth of food after 7pm!

Just typing that makes me want to cry—cry for how I broke the fast and how I really was in the wrong mindset from the beginning; cry because every time I fast, I vow that breaking the fast will be different, that it will be this gracious, "Thank you Jesus" moment rather than the desperate search for food that it always is; and cry because I don't want to do this anymore, this fight. I want to love and serve Jesus, to treat my body as a temple and eat to nourish it, not stuff it for pleasure.

Maybe I wasn't as proficient at fasting as I thought…

This whole experience served two very profound purposes: The first was God's way of letting me know that there is nothing I can do for Him that I can have "down pat" or execute in perfect proficiency on my own. If I think I can "do God's work" on autopilot, then I'm not doing God's work, I'm doing Sandra's work. I need to be fully relying on God to do His work; it shouldn't be an easy walk-in-the-park experience. If it's easy, I better step aside and look at which park I'm in, because it's most likely the wrong one.

Secondly, I need to be aware of the things that lead me off God's path. God guides me in the direction I need to go, but this new direction is fighting old habits and selfish desires that have been ingrained in me for a long time. Old habits come back so easily when I'm doing things without His help. These habits lead me astray most often. My ways of doing things for me and my gains are always going to try to trump doing things for God and His glory when I am relying on me and not God.

Oswald Chambers sums it up like this in My Utmost For His Highest (October 24): "We are not on display in God's showcase - we are here to exhibit only one thing–'the capacity [of our lives] to the obedience of Christ' (2 Corinthians 10:5)... We should belong so completely to the Victor that it is always His Victory, and 'we are more than conquerors through Him...'(Romans 8:37)."

As I reflect on these words and the ones I have written, I realize there are not specific experiences that this applies to, but my entire life. God is changing and growing every part of me throughout every day. That means every part of every day I need to say, "You drive this life Jesus. You drive." It will keep me from weeble-wobbling through this world and on a straight path to glorifying Him.

> AS A PRISONER FOR THE LORD THEN, I URGE YOU TO LIVE A LIFE WORTHY OF THE CALLING YOU HAVE RECEIVED. BE COMPLETELY HUMBLE AND GENTLE; BE PATIENT BEARING WITH ONE ANOTHER WITH LOVE.
>
> EPHESIANS 4:1,2

> THIS IS WHAT THE LORD SAYS: 'LET NOT THE WISE MAN BOAST OF HIS WISDOM OR THE STRONG MAN OF HIS STRENGTH OR THE RICH MAN OF HIS RICHES, BUT LET HIM WHO BOAST, BOAST ABOUT THIS: THAT HE UNDERSTANDS AND KNOWS ME, THAT I AM THE LORD, WHO EXERCISES KINDNESS, JUSTICE, AND RIGHTEOUSNESS ON EARTH, FOR IN THESE I DELIGHT,' DECLARES THE LORD.
>
> JEREMIAH 9:23-24

SIXTEEN
Defined

> We are therefore Christ's ambassadors, as though God were making his appeal through us. We implore you on Christ's behalf: Be reconciled to God. God made him who had no sin to be sin for us, so that in him we might become the righteousness of God.
>
> 2 Corinthians 5:20-21

Balance

Balance. It's one of the most important things you need to ride a bike on two wheels, and it is something three of my four children have. Once my five-year-old daughter started riding her bike without training wheels, she had no problem keeping up with the "big" kids.

And while we were equally excited my five-year-old son was riding his own bike, we couldn't quite convince him to give up his training wheels. He also had no desire to keep up with the big kids, but preferred his pace, which is stop-and-smell-the-roses slow. I asked him when he might want to take his training wheels off, to which he promptly replied, "When I am ten."

I can't say I blame him. Riding with the extra wheels makes it easier to balance and work the bike up and down the hills. They also give him the ability to stop and just sit on his bike when he gets tired or needs a rest. But they are coming off, and it will be a lot sooner than when he is ten.

I have recently been feeling a similar message—a time-to-take-the-training-wheels-off message, meaning God wants me to get my balance with Him.

"Balance" is the word God has had people speaking into my life lately. And there are two very distinct ways He wants me to achieve it:

The first is in what I'm doing in life—activities, time with Him, time alone, rest, family time, community, etc., making sure all the components I need to thrive for Jesus are there in the right amounts.

They haven't been recently, which is why He's calling me back to it. I've been forsaking rest the most, which causes me to get run down and start letting things that are important to God and my health fall through the cracks. Compound that with overcommitting myself, and the result is an unbalanced schedule. So God decided He would provide me some rest and time to accomplish what He was calling me to.

I had two days where I had to cancel everything because I had sick kids. The Internet was down all week too. So I was homebound with nothing to do but love my children, sit with God, and rest. He pulled me out of the unbalanced chaos into a place of complete surrender to what He had planned for me. It was such a blessing to have to sit in my house without Internet and trust that God was in control.

While at home resting, God reminded me that I'm not only called to balance my schedule, but to balance everything I do with Him.

When I was a school teacher, I took a survey once that was supposed to indicate the "balance of activities" I have in my life. The survey listed several activities in a circle with the numbers 0 through 10 radiating out from the center of the circle to each activity. I distinctly remember when taking the survey that mine was almost a complete circle–all my answers were 7s, 8s, or 9s except one–which made my survey look like it was a pie with a missing piece.

The piece I was missing was "Spirituality"—I scored a 2 in that category because I was not walking with the Lord at that time. As I reflect on this exercise now, God is opening my eyes to view it differently. He is not just a piece of my life. He is the pie plate that

Chapter Sixteen - Defined

everything is to be placed upon.

If the base of everything I do is Jesus, it is begun and run on a firm foundation. But before I even place things on Him, I need to make sure it is held to His standards, not the world's.

In 1 Kings 22, the king of Israel, Ahab, wants Jehoshaphat to fight a war with him. Before Jehoshaphat will do this, he wants to consult the LORD. So Ahab brings forth all his prophets, and I say "his" here, because these were not Godly men, but men who told Ahab what he wanted to hear, so they came forth and all said that, yes, proceeding into war is exactly what the kings should do. But Jehoshaphat doesn't buy it. He wants a prophet from God and asks Ahab if he has any of those and Ahab's reply is: "There is still one man through whom we can inquire of the LORD, but I hate him because he never prophesies anything good about me, but always bad." (1 Kings 22:8).

The one guy that is going to give him the truth he doesn't want to hear from, because the truth isn't going to get him what he wants. His advisors (the world) have told him that what he is going to do is good—he has support for his plan and trusts in himself, but his plan is neither supported by the Lord nor is it looked at through the Lord's standards. It's all him, so when the prophet comes and says negative things about Ahab, Ahab just says, "See!" to Jehoshaphat, meaning this one opinion must be wrong, encouraging Jehoshaphat to go to war anyway.

God is calling me to do the same to not balance my life with things of Him *and* things of the world. He wants all things in my life to be of Him and held to His standards. He wants to help me, support me, and glorify Himself through all I am doing, but He does not do that when I am focused on the world.

God never wants me to take on the burden of something alone. He has graciously offered His shoulders, time and time again; He gives me the Bible as a guidebook to teach me what pleases him; He has equipped me to balance on just two wheels; I have to show my trust by lifting my feet up and balancing it all with Him.

Nakedness

ALL A MAN'S WAYS SEEM RIGHT TO HIM, BUT THE LORD WEIGHS THE HEART.

PROVERBS 21:2

BE CAREFUL, OR YOUR HEARTS WILL BE WEIGHED DOWN WITH DISSIPATION, DRUNKENNESS AND THE ANXIETIES OF LIFE, AND THAT DAY WILL CLOSE ON YOU UNEXPECTEDLY LIKE A TRAP. FOR IT WILL COME UPON ALL WHO LIVE ON THE FACE OF THE WHOLE EARTH. BE ALWAYS ON THE WATCH, AND PRAY THAT YOU MAY BE ABLE TO ESCAPE ALL THAT IS ABOUT TO HAPPEN, AND THAT YOU MAY BE ABLE TO STAND BEFORE THE SON OF MAN.

LUKE 21:34-36

Intimacy

My husband and I have a lot of sex. Now you may feel that is too much information, but I don't, and let me tell you why. Sex is a mainstream topic that seems OK to discuss on the T.V., to show in movies, and talk about and participate in if you are single. But rarely do you hear married people talk about sex—the one place it should be talked about all the time.

Sex, between a married man and a woman, is not only a form of companionship and procreation, but also displays to us the intimate relationship and amazing love Jesus has for you and me (the "church"). It is also a reminder of the promise that my husband and I made with God when we got married, to represent this loving relationship through our interaction with each other.

As a married woman, when I think of sex, through God's eyes—making love to my husband becomes more than a physical interaction—it is emotional and intimate achieving an amazing connection between us. A connection that comes from our love for each other that is rooted in our love of God, something we could never achieve on our own.

Nakedness

This is a new way of thinking for me as I had too much sex growing up, so by the time I was married, it was no longer an emotional intimate act, but a burden and a chore. Now, after many years of praying for desire and enjoyment, sermons I have heard, and books I have read, I can say that sex is becoming what God intended it to be in my life.

I realized how my thoughts were changing to this new way of thinking during a recent lull my husband and I have been in. He's been traveling and has been sick and I've been busy writing a book and raising four kids—both of us preoccupied with all that is going on in life, creating a lack of time for each other.

I found that since we weren't carving out the time to get intimate, it was leading to a feeling of disconnect. There's no doubt or worry that my husband and I love each other and are meant to be together. There is just this feeling of something missing in our relationship.

And for me to acknowledge that sex is the missing thing is huge. Due to the amount of past experience baggage I brought into our relationship, I had previously not been the one to initiate sex, in fact I would say that I would actually try to avoid it. But now, because of what God has done in my heart, I love and crave our intimacy and yearn for it when it is not there.

Our time together is so much more than the physical. It is our special moment to talk, to listen, to pray, to get a reprieve. We truly reconnect during our time with one another.

There are so many things that pull my husband and I away from our marriage—kids, work, life—that if we are not intentional about locking the door and "getting away" with each other, there is the possibility we could drift apart. It breaks my heart to think that would happen, and I am so thankful to God for opening my eyes to this and putting the desire in my heart to make time to get cozy with my husband.

God has laid this on my heart to encourage you to pursue God and this intimacy in your marriage—to remember that this is not a burden, a chore, or something to be neglected, something to

Chapter Sixteen - Defined

be abused or make amends. Instead, it is a gift and a reminder of something greater than us. I hope to spur you on to not take your spouse for granted, but take the time to reconnect and show the love of Christ to each other.

And if you've never been married, I pray that you would cherish and save this gift that God has blessed you with until He brings the right person along with whom to share it.

> HUSBANDS, LOVE YOUR WIVES JUST AS CHRIST LOVED THE CHURCH AND GAVE HIMSELF UP FOR HER TO MAKE HER HOLY, CLEANSING HER BY THE WASHING WITH WATER THROUGH THE WORD, AND TO PRESENT HER TO HIMSELF AS A RADIANT CHURCH, WITHOUT STAIN OR WRINKLE OR ANY OTHER BLEMISH, BUT HOLY AND BLAMELESS.
>
> EPHESIANS 5:25-27

> DO NOT DEPRIVE EACH OTHER EXCEPT BY MUTUAL CONSENT FOR A TIME, SO THAT YOU MAY DEVOTE YOURSELVES TO PRAYER. THEN COME TOGETHER AGAIN SO THAT SATAN WILL NOT TEMPT YOU BECAUSE OF YOUR LACK OF SELF-CONTROL.
>
> 1 CORINTHIANS 7:5

Bullied

My oldest son is being bullied at his elementary school. There is a boy in his class who says inappropriate things, kicks him when he gets a drink at the water fountain, and follows my son around at recess taunting him, making school life uncomfortable and unpleasant.

My husband and I have tried to arm my son with so many different tactics, some peaceful, some not, and have even brought the teacher, principal, vice principal, and counselor into the situation . . . to no avail. The bullying continues and my son is being overtaken with the helpless sensation that nothing is being done at school. At home, I can see how my sweet boy's confidence and self-esteem are slowly being picked away, and we're left unsure of what to do.

As I told a friend about this she immediately said, "Let's pray right now." We held hands and she began with: "Heavenly Father, we lift this bully up to you." I admit, after she said that phrase I stopped thinking about what she was praying for, and for a split second could only think about my kid. *What about my kid? Why is she praying for the bully?* was my thought process, followed by: She's praying for the enemy here!

Chapter Sixteen - Defined

Yes, she was, and that was exactly what I needed her to do to get my focus back to where it needed to be. I had gotten so caught up in protecting my child and the frustration on how the situation was being handled, I had forgotten to trust God and to keep my eyes on Him.

It was important for me to handle this God's way and not mine because of the interaction I had already had with the bully's mom. After I sent an email to my son's class, the bully's mom responded with concern for me because I always sign my e-mails with some kind of statement of faith: "God bless you" or "Have a blessed day." She was worried about me receiving backlash in such a diverse community.

I prayed about my response and then wrote her back, and this is basically what I said: I let her know that since Jesus has opened my eyes to His love for me, it is hard to keep the joy quiet. How could I possibly remain silent about the fact that Jesus died on the cross for my sins, rose from the grave on the third day, and now stands in heaven being my ambassador before God?

I never heard from her again.

But it's not important what her response was because now she knows I love Jesus. Now she knows Who I represent, so my reaction to the bullying situation and how I handle it needs to reflect the love Jesus has given me. I can't enter into this situation full of my flesh nature with my typical earthly reactions like frustration and anger—both of which are acceptable emotions when expressed for the right reasons, but that was the trick.

When my emotions are serving God's purpose, I need to exude them with the passion and fervor the Almighty has given me. But when I am expressing myself to serve my selfish purpose, I need to re-evaluate and redirect the source of my energy. In this situation, my emotions were self-driven. My response needed to be humble and represent the truth that Jesus loved the lost and the broken.

I have proclaimed myself as a follower of Christ, my actions need to do the same. Especially in these circumstances, where God has made it clear to me that this situation is about Him—not me, my son, or even the bully, but God and His abundant love for His children.

When I see the bullying situation from the eyes of Jesus, it changes the issue from protecting my child to getting this bully help; to praying for him and his parents and supporting them through this tough time. The bully's mom knew I loved Jesus, now I was charged to respond to her and her family with the same grace and love He has given me.

Through all this I can hold on to that fact that God is in absolute control—He is Sovereign. He can protect and love my son much better than I can. The bully situation is not resolved, but ongoing. But God is in control and using all of it for not only my good, but also for the good of my son, the bully, and hopefully every other person involved too.

> **Be careful, however, that the exercise of your rights does not become a stumbling block to the weak.**
>
> **1 Corinthians 8:9**

> **We are therefore Christ's ambassadors, as though God were making his appeal through us. We implore you on Christ's behalf: Be reconciled to God. God made him who had no sin to be sin for us, so that in him we might become the righteousness of God.**
>
> **2 Corinthians 5:20-21**

SEVENTEEN
Revelation

Therefore, since we are surrounded by such a great cloud of witnesses, let us throw off everything that hinders and the sin that so easily entangles, and let us run with perseverance the race marked out for us. Let us fix our eyes on Jesus, the author and perfecter of our faith, who for the joy set before him endured the cross, scorning its shame, and sat down at the right hand of God. Consider him who endured such opposition from sinful men, so that you will not grow weary and lose heart.

Hebrews 12:1-3

Overcomer

Whenever I go skiing, I'm very reliant on Jesus. I don't ski very well, so as I go down the mountain it's with much prayer and great dependence on the Lord and His host of angels to get me to the bottom in one piece. There are some slopes I go down that require a little more help from Jesus than others, like the one my husband and I accidentally ended up on during a ski trip one year.

If you have never been skiing before, you need to know that the mountain slopes are labeled in different colors and symbols to indicate the difficulty of the slope: green circles are the easiest/beginner slopes; blue squares are for intermediate; and black diamond and double-black diamond are for advanced skiers. My husband and I ski green- and blue-colored slopes.

For our last run of the day, when we were tired and ready to go in, we chose a path down the mountain that we had not gone on before that was marked blue. Unfortunately, we made a wrong turn and ended up on a black diamond slope. This particular slope was a straight-down shot with huge moguls (big bumps) all the way down the slope. There was a nice leveling out and then another straight-down shot with bigger moguls.

Nakedness

We decided to try to get away from the moguls by cutting through the forest to the next slope over, but it turned out to have even bigger moguls than the one we left. So with much fear and trepidation, we inched down the hill.

I talked to Jesus the entire time, asking for Him to help, praying for protection, knowing that there was no way I was getting off this mountain without Him. The going was slow, but we eventually made it to another leveling-out area where we could get to a different slope that was a blue. Praise God neither of us had broken limbs, and to both our surprise, didn't fall.

That night I thought about how I had overcome this huge mountain pass only by fully relying on Jesus. There was no way I could have gotten down without the Lord, and let me tell you why: about halfway down this mogul-filled slope, I looked at where I had to go and felt tears well up in my eyes.

The impossibility of the situation had begun to overwhelm me, and I was ready to give up. It was here that I felt an assurance in my heart that Jesus was with me all the way and He would help me overcome this situation. Which He did.

I looked at this opportunity for me to overcome a great physical challenge as a reminder that I can trust Him to help me prevail over the greater spiritual and emotional struggles I continue to face.

For example, I still use food for so much more than nourishment, and it still holds a greater place in my heart than Jesus. Ouch. Jesus has offered His plan to help me get beyond this food issue, but I don't want to do what He asks, so I turn to a gluten-free toasted English muffin instead.

Or there are other times I fully embrace the guidance Jesus offers, and what begins with a yes-I-will attitude ends with tears in my eyes and impossibility in my heart because I've taken Jesus and His plan out and replaced it with me and my plan. Despite all this, Jesus continues to always be there, just like He was on the mountain, wanting me to overcome and fully trust in Him.

Chapter Seventeen - Revelation

And the word "overcome" has so much hope wrapped up in it for me. I yearn to be an overcomer—not just a person who succeeds at something, but the overcomer the Bible talks about. I can make it through a challenge and say that I have overcome, but to overcome Biblically is to prevail empowered by Jesus. The only part that is mine in overcoming Biblically is to stop trying to do it myself and trust Jesus to do it.

A great example that really hit home with me is in Max Lucado's wonderful children's story called *You Are Special*. It is the story of the Wemmicks, who are wooden people, each individually carved by the woodcarver, Eli.

The Wemmicks spend their days sticking gray dot and gold star stickers on each other according to their looks and accomplishments. If you are pretty or do something good, you get a gold star. If you are not carved as nicely and can't do much, you get a gray dot.

The story focuses on one particular Wemmick named Punchinello, who can't seem to get anything right so he gets lots of gray dots; which eventually causes him to believe that he is not a good Wemmick. One day, he meets a Wemmick who has no stars or dots. Her name is Lucia. He asks her why she has no stickers, and she says she spends some time every day with Eli their maker and suggests he do the same.

Punchinello gets up the courage to go see Eli and ask Him about why the dots don't stick to Lucia. Eli says, "Because she has decided that what I think is more important than what they think. The stickers only stick if they matter to you. The more you trust my love, the less you care about their stickers." As Punchinello digests this and turns to leave, he is reminded by Eli that he is special because Eli made him and that Eli doesn't make mistakes. Punchinello thinks he believes what Eli is saying as he walks out the door, and a gray dot falls off.

Lucia is the overcomer—she cares not what the world or her fellow Wemmicks think of her, but only what her maker believes her to be. She is able to overcome this situation only because she spends time with Eli every day. Punchinello is on his way to overcoming his thought that other Wemmicks define who he is; and that only happens when he begins to believe the truth that the only opinion that matters is his maker's.

The key in this story and my life, to being an overcomer, is not about defeating or prevailing over whatever challenge is in my path, but about how I am empowered to do it. Both of these overcoming Wemmicks succeed because they spend time with their maker every day and let His words ring as truth in their hearts.

Why is it so hard for me to trust and believe that Jesus can empower me to overcome? Because it means I would have to forget my old habits and live the new; to care only what Jesus thinks and not the world; to live focused on the Lord—all things I yearn to do but can't do on my own and haven't quite surrendered them to Jesus completely, yet.

Don't get me wrong, I believe I'm on my way to being an overcomer. I feel like I'm Punchinello and that as I do embrace a new truth that God opens my eyes to, a dot falls off. It just all happens through this journey called life and I'd rather it all happen right now.

Because who wouldn't want to be an overcomer? Look at all God promises in the last book of the Bible, Revelation:

> The overcomer is given "the right to eat from the tree of life, which is in the paradise of God." (2:7)

> The overcomer "will not be hurt at all by the second death." (2:11)

> The overcomer will be given "some of the hidden manna" and will be given "a white stone and a new name written on it." (2:17)
>
> The overcomer will be given "authority over the nations" and "the morning star." (2:26)
>
> The overcomer "will be dressed in white" and "never blot out his name from the book of life, but acknowledge his name before my Father and His angels." (3:5)
>
> The overcomer will be made a "pillar in the temple of my God. Never again will he leave it," and written on him will be "the name of my God and the name of the city of my God, the new Jerusalem," (3:12)
>
> The overcomer will be given "the right to sit with me (Jesus) on my throne, just as I (Jesus) overcame and sat down with my Father on His throne." (3:21)

I will continue to desire to be an overcomer. And the best part is this is God's desire for me too. He is there every step of the way to guide me through the tough terrain when I reach for Him. He is there in the mundane moments of my day waiting for me to talk to Him. He is there throughout the chaos that surrounds my schedule, wanting me to hold tight to Him rather than what I think my life should look like. He is there through it all.

Still, even though He is there, He always gives me a choice. God is all knowing and has ordained all my days, so I should follow Him. He created me with His purpose in mind, so I should listen to Him. God has shown me His magnificent glory and how He deserves my worship through His Word, so I should worship Him. God exemplifies His Sovereignty and dependability as I live out daily life, so I should trust Him. I should, but often times, I don't. But when I do, He empowers me to overcome.

As you can tell, I have a long way to go. My journey is only beginning. And while God has a lot more things to strip away, my hope remains in the greatest Overcomer that ever walked the earth. Let me encourage you with a description of this Overcomer.

Jesus came in complete humility. He was the Creator and came to earth as His creation, laying aside His glory so that He could serve the very people He created. He was tempted beyond anything we will ever endure, and then died the death for sins He didn't commit.

Finally, He rose from the grave to overcome death and sin forever. Jesus overcame all sin as He lived His life, and then overcame death through His resurrection. This Ultimate Overcomer empowers me and you to prevail and succeed, not by our own doing, but by His. Praise God!

> I have told you things so that in me you may have peace. In this world you will have trouble. But take heart! I have overcome the world.
>
> John 16:33

> This is how we know that we love the children of God: by loving God and carrying out His commands. This is love for God: to obey His commands and His commands are not burdensome, for everyone born of God overcomes the world. This is the victory that has overcome the world, even our faith. Who is it that overcomes the world? Only he who believes that Jesus is the Son of God.
>
> 1 John 5:2-5

Afterword

Do you know anyone who reads the last page of the book first? My son does this and it drives me crazy! I used to struggle to understand why you would want to find out how a story ends instead of letting the story develop and take you where it may, until I read the Bible.

Before I read the Bible from cover to cover, I was encouraged by friends to read the last page first, and now I understand. The ending offers the hope, love, and victory that are proclaimed throughout the book. I see that by knowing the ending, it gives a safety net to persevere through the beginning and middle or, in my case, to trudge through the mundane and run through the chaos with new perspective and encouragement.

Maybe you are doing this right now with this book—reading the last page first. If so, I encourage you to go back to the beginning, because even though the brokenness and imperfections you find here at the end are the same as the ones that you will find at the beginning, you have missed the important journey in the middle.

If you have arrived at this page because you have cried with me and laughed at me and hopefully seen a little bit of God through my experiences, then I pray that you will embrace your own journey—the unique journey that God has you on.

I pray that you will strip away the things you used to hide behind and let the world see that you are not perfect, but there is Someone whose perfection shines through you. I pray that God grabs hold of your heart in such a mighty way that it brings you to your knees and tears to your eyes.

I pray that you see the mighty sacrifice Jesus made on your behalf, and that, maybe, you could sacrifice a little for Him.

I pray that you encourage another with the comfort God has given you and that maybe, just maybe, you and I can both be a little more naked in the light of God's love from now on.

By His divine power, God has given us everything we need for living a godly life. We have received all this by coming to know Him, the one who calls us to himself by means of His marvelous glory and excellence.

2 Peter 1:3

I pray that out of his glorious riches he may strengthen you with power through his Spirit in your inner being, so that Christ may dwell in your hearts through faith. And I pray that you, being rooted and established in love, may have power, together with all the Lord's holy people, to grasp how wide and long and high and deep is the love of Christ, and to know this love that surpasses knowledge—that you may be filled to the measure of all the fullness of God.

Ephesians 3:16-19

Acknowledgments

"Whatever you do, do for the glory of God." I wouldn't have been able to write this book if it were not for the Lord, and so I must give credit where it belongs, and thank Him for this humbling, challenging, and joyful adventure. I am so grateful to God that I have been blessed with this opportunity to share this journey with you and give Him all the glory for it.

While God sent me out on this journey, He did not ask me to go alone, but surrounded me with wonderful family, friends, prayer warriors, and Sisters in Christ. I am so grateful for their words, prayers, encouragement, and help, in bringing this book to fruition.

I am grateful for my children, who provided me countless experiences and reflections to write about, as well as invaluable lessons that can only be seen through the eyes of a child.

I am grateful to my publisher, Kent Gustavson, for taking the time to understand the journey I am on, and offering his wisdom and vision to help me portray that to the world through a book.

I am grateful for my sweet friend Debbie Collins, who copy-edited every new version on a short time frame and gave me her priceless insight each time.

I am grateful for my sister-in-law, Elizabeth Anne Moore of Elizabeth Anne Photography, for her amazing eye to see the hidden beauty in everything and her incredible talent for being able to capture it in a picture, just as she did for the cover of this book.

I am grateful for Andy and Lynn Neillie who believed in me enough to connect me with their publisher and offered incredible, constant encouragement to pursue the path God has put me on.

I am grateful for Beau Landrum, Don Ramer, and Heidi Harrod, fellow authors and friends who invested their time, ideas, and input into this book.

I am grateful for my Sister in Christ, Karen Moore, who knew exactly what I needed help with, even before I asked—for watching my children on numerous occassions so I could do what I needed to get done; for reading multiple versions of this book and offering her valuable insight.

I am grateful to the pastors and staff at Austin Stone Community Church, who are bold enough to proclaim the Truth and live transparent lives—encouraging me to do the same.

CONCORDANCE

Genesis 2:25 (14)
Genesis 3:7 (14)
Genesis 50:20 (203)
Exodus 15:2 (114)
Deuteronomy 6:5-9 (137)
Deuteronomy 8:3 (105)
Deuteronomy 11:18-20 (201)
Judges 2:10 (111)
1 Samuel 15 (186)
1 Samuel 17 (180)
2 Samuel 12:7b, 8 (89)
1 Kings 22:8 (215)
Psalm 18:1,2 (86)
Psalm 19:8 (86)
Psalm 27:1 (40)
Psalm 37:5, 6 (51)
Psalm 46:1 (92)
Psalm 46:10 (92)
Psalm 119:133 (187)
Psalm 130:5,6 (115)
Psalm 139:7-10 (83)
Proverbs 3:5, 6 (60)
Proverbs 15:1 (86)
Proverbs 20:24 (43)
Proverbs 21:2 (216)
Isaiah 40:31 (181)
Isaiah 41:10 (153)
Jeremiah 1:19 (101)
Jeremiah 9:23,24 (208)
Jeremiah 29:11 (71)
Daniel 1:3-6,8-16 (150)
Daniel 2:20-22 (63)
Daniel 4:34b, 35 (98)
Daniel 4:37 (63)
Daniel 9:20-23 (168)
Micah 6:6-8 (99)
Matthew 4:1-11 (103)
Matthew 6:33, 34 (205)
Matthew 7:4,5 (60)
Matthew 7:13-14 (50)

Matthew 9:13b (98)
Matthew 11:28-30 (197)
Matthew 12:36,37 (164)
Matthew 16:24,25 (102, 175)
Matthew 19:4-6 (24)
Matthew 25:14-30 (76)
Matthew 28:19, 20 (123)
Mark 7:8,9 (168)
Mark 8:35 (193)
Mark 9:35 (175)
Luke 6:37, 38 (143)
Luke 11:24-26 (104)
Luke 18:27 (178)
Luke 21:34-36 (216)
John 3:16,17 (115)
John 3:19 -21 (24)
John 16:33 (232)
Romans 2:1 (164)
Romans 5:8 (113)
Romans 6:20-23 (193)
Romans 7:18, 19 (127)
Romans 7:20 (127)
Romans 8:5-8 (149)
Romans 8:26, 27 (167)
Romans 8:28 (24, 117, 140)
Romans 8:31, 32 (149)
Romans 8:37 (208)
Romans 8:38-39 (75)
Romans 12:2 (189)
Romans 12:6 (78)
Romans 12:9 (128)
1 Corinthians 2:1-5 (190)
1 Corinthians 7:5 (219)
1 Corinthians 8:9 (222)
1 Corinthians 10:12, 13 (36)
1 Corinthians 10:31-11:1 (201)
1 Corinthians 12:4-6 (78)
1 Corinthians 13:4-7, 13 (75)
1 Corinthians 16:13, 14 (205)
2 Corinthians 1:3-4 (19)

2 Corinthians 3:18 (119)
2 Corinthians 4:17,18 (133)
2 Corinthians 5:20, 21 (211, 222)
2 Corinthians 10:5 (208)
2 Corinthians 12:9,10 (113)
Galatians 2:20 (111, 131)
Galatians 6:7b-10a (156)
Ephesians 1:15 (91)
Ephesians 2:3-8 (155)
Ephesians 2:8c (128)
Ephesians 2:9 (155)
Ephesians 2:10 (119)
Ephesians 3:16-19 (236)
Ephesians 4:1,2 (208)
Ephesians 5:8-10 (81)
Ephesians 5:18 (29)
Ephesians 5:25-27 (219)
Ephesians 5:31-33 (36)
Ephesians 6:4 (137)
Ephesians 6:18 (133)
Ephesians 6:19,20 (178)
Philippians 2:3,4 (175)
Philippians 2:5-8 (121, 192)
Philippians 3:16 (159)
Philippians 4:6 (39, 140)
Philippians 4:7 (140)
Philippians 4:11-12 (181)
Philippians 4:13 (29, 68, 181)
Colossians 1:9 (133)
Colossians 1:10,11 (81)
Colossians 2:6,7 (59)
Colossians 2:8 (47, 74)
Colossians 2:20 (131, 153)
Colossians 2:21-23 (153)
Colossians 3:2 (145)
Colossians 3:3 (118, 145)
Colossians 3:17 (183)
Colossians 3:23 (59, 73)
Colossians 4:2 (133)
1 Thessalonians 5:11 (68)

1 Thessalonians 5:16-18 (171)
1 Thessalonians 5:17 (133)
2 Thessalonians 1:11 (133)
2 Thessalonians 2:16,17 (68)
1 Timothy 6:11,12 (89)
2 Timothy 3:16, 17 (95)
Hebrews 3:13, 14 (65)
Hebrews 4:12 (57, 112)
Hebrews 10:23 (107)
Hebrews 10:24 (115)
Hebrews 10:26,27 (143)
Hebrews 12:1-3 (225)
Hebrews 12:28,29 (99)
James 1:4 (49)
James 2:14-17 (56)
James 2:26 (57)
James 4:7 (202)
1Peter 1:8,9 (125)
1Peter 3:18 (187)
1 Peter 4:10-11 (53)
1 Peter 4:12,13 (49)
1 Peter 5:8 (104)
2 Peter 1:3 (236)
1 John 1:8-10 (47)
1 John 2:15 (51, 131)
1 John 2:16 (131)
1 John 4:18 (40)
1 John 5:3,4 (125)
1 John 5:7-9 (232)
3 John 11 (190)
Revelation 2:7,11,17,26 (230, 231)
Revelation 3:5, 12 (231)
Revelation 3:21 (231)
Revelation 8 (112)
Revelation 9:16-19 (127)
Revelation 13 (142)
Revelation 19:11-16 (80)
Revelation 22:7 (105)

About the Author

Sandra Kristen Moore was born and raised near Chicago before leaving to study at Truman State University. She met her husband Rob there, and moved with him to Austin, Texas, where they still live with their four children and two dogs. She began writing a weekly devotional in 2007 because of the significant way she felt her life beginning to change as she pursued a relationship with God. She has found great meaning through ministering to her family, helping her community, and sharing her journey with others. Find out more at http://www.sandrakristenmoore.com

Made in the USA
San Bernardino, CA
21 November 2013